The **LOST** *Kingdom*

gateway to your inheritance

Adrian Beale

ADRIAN BEALE

PO Box 87 HOPE VALLEY, SOUTH AUSTRALIA 5090

ISBN 978-0-9875915-1-7

Reach me on the web www.everrestministries.com
Follow me on Facebook and Instagram @adrianbeale

Acknowledgments

Special thanks to Rhonda Pooley and my daughter Rebekah Beale. Rhonda for proof reading and correcting the original manuscript and to Bek for helping me develop artwork, typesetting and illustrating the final document.

Thanks to all my friends and ministries whose questions encouraged me to complete this volume.

Key to Annotations

cf. compare
eg. for example
f. verse or page that follows
ff. verses or pages following
ie. that is
NB Note well
NT New Testament
OT Old Testament
TSOTM The Sermon on the Mount

This book is meant to be read, highlighted, underlined, digested and applied in the areas where Holy Spirit speaks to you.

Contents

Diagrams

Endorsements

I have been looking forward to reading this book and enjoyed it even more than anticipated. Adrian is a true five-fold teacher and every time he speaks, whether in passing conversation or in a teaching setting I want to take notes. In reading this book, I was so encouraged to hear the Holy Spirit speaking so many of the same things for this time that He has been sharing with me, and with Adrian's special gift as a prophetic teacher, my heart is lit up with revelation and excitement. This is a book you will want to read and re-read because it is rich with revelation that provides prophetic insight, sparking the hearts to feed on the truths contained in it.

Katherine Ruonala
Author: "Living in the Miraculous: How God's love is expressed through the Supernatural" and "Wilderness to Wonders - Embracing the power of process"
Senior Leader of Glory City Church and Glory City International Network.
Founder and Facilitator of the Australian Prophetic Council

The Lost Kingdom serves as an invaluable tool to help us better understand how to operate within a functional Kingdom paradigm as sons of God here on Earth. Adrian displays an incredible command of the Hebraic origin of many scriptures as he takes us on a journey into empowering truths that are sure to equip and release many into a new level of administrating the Kingdom of Heaven through their lives. This book is designed to provoke, inspire and activate all who read it. An important read for the Body of Christ at this time.

Daryl Crawford-Marshall
Founder DCM Ministries

I want to highly recommend the latest book, The Lost Kingdom by my friend Adrian Beale. In a generation filled with clichés and seeker sensitive Christian ideas this book is a breathe of fresh air to those who are truly hungry for the Kingdom of God. Adrian's theological and scholarly approach to scripture as well as fresh revelation concerning the Kingdom of God will help bring great insight into the mysteries of the Living Word, Jesus Christ to you as a believer. If you're ready to step beyond the borders of status quo Christianity and into the world of the Kingdom this is a must have book.

Charlie Shamp
Founder and President
Destiny Encounters International
www.destinyencounters.com

Adrian Beale is a true 'son of the kingdom.' Jesus revealed that His ultimate desire was to send forth "sons of the kingdom" into the world. These are the good seed that He desires to sow into the world. "He who sows the good seed is the Son of Man. The field is the world; the good seeds are the sons of the kingdom." (Matthew 13:37,38) To see this kingdom, we must be born again. Once we can see it we are challenged to receive it and to choose to fully enter it. It is only once we have received it that we can give it away. The path of discipleship is the path of receiving and giving the kingdom. Disciples of the kingdom become kingdom carriers who can release the glory of the kingdom of heaven on earth. This forerunner book outlines the path of receiving the kingdom and joining the Father in his good pleasure to give it away. Adrian takes his readers on a revelatory journey into seeing the kingdom everywhere throughout the Word of God. I have a passion for good kingdom theology that invites us to become partakers of the glory realm of heaven. This book is an excellent invitation to join the prophetic journey of discovering the hidden dimensions of heaven invading earth. I heartily commend this book to those who desire deeper revelation into God's glorious purposes in these last days.

Phil Mason
Spiritual Director
Tribe, Byron Bay
Australia
www.tribebyronbay.com

There is a resurgence today of prophetic voices that are bringing Kingdom awareness and ability for the purpose of partnering with the Godhead in the discipling of nations. It is our Father's deep passion to have a company of believers that fully measure up to the stature of Christ and who are found faithfully advancing the kingdom and occupying every realm of society when Christ returns. In order for this to transpire the body of Christ will need to pick up what has been lost; that is the Kingdom message and it's clarion call to fully possess our promise-land.

I believe Adrian Beale is one of these prophetic voices who has a unique assignment to call the church to see all of life through Kingdom lenses.

Adrian sees the strength of revelation as "the substance of the kingdom and the treasure hid in a field." He contends that all of scripture is awaiting us to discover what is hidden underneath; that we have an invitation to use scripture as the very means to enter another realm. I have personally seen the intense joy on Adrian's face as he recounts his own journey of discovering hidden secrets and I know that as you read this book you can receive this same anointing to pursue a life of Kingdom revelation.

As the church goes beyond a casual relationship with the Holy Scriptures and dives deeply into a Kingdom revelatory mindset we will receive all the answers, all the wisdom, all the strength and all the resources we need to advance His Kingdom.

I have often said to my church, "an hour of kingdom meditation is equal to a 100 hours of toil".

So with that in mind I heartily recommend "The lost kingdom" to you. I pray that as you read this book you will receive a fresh anointing and hunger to pursue the skills of meditation, revelation and prophetic speaking, for it is in these keys that the joy of Kingdom partnership, acceleration and supernatural increase are birthed in our lives.

Andrew Magrath
Senior Pastor: Hope City Church Melbourne
Author: The gospel according to Noah

Wow ... not only is this beautifully written it is an invitation to come up higher and dig deeper.

Adrian is not presenting his own finite revelation but opening every readers spiritual eyes to their own remarkable, unique fresh revelation gift wrapped in the covers of this book.

We recommend this to you knowing as you read you will be inspired. Congratulations Adrian!

Paul and Pamela Segneri
Founders Integrity Restoration Ministries and FirestartersTV

Many times in the last 50 plus years, the Body of Christ has attempted to 'cross over' into the 'Promised Land'. Yet it appears that too many are still 'wandering in the wilderness' — just getting by with 'manna'. Adrian reveals the "missing link" of the revelation of the Kingdom of God in his book, the Lost Kingdom.

Stephen Strader
Senior Pastor Ignited Church
Lakeland Florida

Introduction

It has become increasing apparent to me as I have been called upon to preach the gospel of the kingdom throughout the world that very little is understood in the Body of Christ about the two-fold nature of the cross. Whereas Jesus death in payment for our sins and the redemption that it bought is an ingrained reality to the vast majority of believers, when those same believers are asked what the kingdom looks like or how it is entered, the room suddenly goes eerily silent. There is therefore a much weighted mismatch of understanding between the cross and the kingdom it established among believers.

As the environment in which we grow is a shaper and precursor to our adult identity, there is an obvious need to regularly present a tangible framework of the kingdom to maturing saints. The absence of such teaching feeds the discord between personal circumstance and our position 'in Christ'. Putting that in a positive light, if we are brought up with the invisible kingdom as our reality we will more readily step into accessing and accepting its provision as sons.

This book is part of a greater move in the Body of Christ to right the scales.

Please be aware that in writing I do not want to rehash someone else's work but simply seek to explore and present what I believe to be Holy Spirit inspired material as a catalyst for transformation. This is perhaps an outlook captured best in the words of George Bernard Shaw,

'The reasonable man adapts himself to the world,
the unreasonable one persists to adapt the world to himself.
Therefore all progress depends on the unreasonable man.'

George Bernard Shaw

CHAPTER ONE

Between Two Worlds

As the clergyman listened to her life story his thoughts wandered to how young and energetic she once must have been. Now with the last chapter of her life drawing to a close she lay before him weathered and exhausted, a mere shadow of her former self. With focus he lent in to embrace and participate in the oral sketches that characterised and unwound something of the life represented before him. As her staccato breaths interposed with memories of joy with her children his attention was drawn over his spectacles to that which hung framed on her bedroom wall just above the dresser. It was its irregularity that caught his attention; the dark timber frame was glaringly disproportionate to what it encased. Now entombed in timber and glass and hidden in this private room with little light were five or so lines of quilled freehand writing etched onto a tattered parchment that betrayed its journey. Not wanting to break the flow of her words he waited and chose his moment to enquire about its meaning. She willingly sauntered on to the new trail and unfolded its origin. It was something she held dear for it came from a previous employer who was held in great esteem. With the change of subject he was now free to stand and take a closer look at what was penned. As he took in its content it was as though a wave of injustice hit him. There in the privacy of this illiterate poor widow's bedroom all this time had been the means to drastically change what had been her final years. The parchment was the last will and testament of her previous proprietor who had bequeathed all to her as his faithful servant. The stark contrast with what might have been immediately struck him. She had been effectively blinded to all that was rightly hers simply through her illiteracy! *This story is attributed to a visit by Charles Haddon Spurgeon (1834-1892) to a dying parishioner, (embellished by the author).*

The Two-Fold Nature of Redemption

I began my first session at a recent conference in Melbourne Australia by asking the audience, 'Why did Jesus die on the cross?' As expected, the audience shouted out things like, 'To atone for our sin!', 'For forgiveness!', 'To reconcile man and God!' 'To fulfil what was written!' 'To fulfil all righteousness!' Every one of these answers is correct and as good Evangelical Christians these have become engrafted into our psyche. For the most part there is no problem with this aspect of our understanding. However, I believe this dimension of Jesus' sacrifice has been so heavily spoken on, it has become entrenched into our thinking to the point that it is as if we are wearing blinders (blinkers) over our eyes preventing us from seeing the rest of the panorama that lies before us (See footnote). In the book of Colossians Paul writes,

'Giving thanks unto the Father, which has made us meet to be partakers of the inheritance of the saints in light:
Who has delivered us from the power of darkness, and has translated us into the kingdom of his dear Son:
In whom we have redemption through His blood, even the forgiveness of sins.'

Colossians 1:12-14

These verses reveal that there is a two-fold consequence to Jesus' death on the cross; His actions not only atoned for our sin and bought our redemption, but also gained entry for us into the kingdom of God! This kingdom is not, as some may think, just an

Footnote: I have asked this same question in more than a dozen churches spread over three continents, all of which profess to be kingdom-oriented congregations. The result has been exactly the same in every one of them. If you are in leadership, without pre-conditioning those you lead, please feel free to ask them the same question: Why did Jesus die on the cross? You may be equally challenged by the result.

14

awaiting utopia, but is also a realm that is here today for those who have had their spiritual senses awakened to see and enter it.

The Kingdom's Timing

How do we know it is here now? Well, Daniel the prophet gave us its timing when he explained to Nebuchadnezzar that God was going to set up a kingdom in the days of '*these kings*' (1). While highly interpretive the four kingdoms described in the context of Daniel's revelation are generally agreed upon to be Babylon, Persia, Greece and Rome. Though there is much conjecture about this passage this understanding of its timing is reinforced by the prophet Isaiah who associated the establishment of the kingdom with the birth of a child called, '*Wonderful, Counselor, The mighty God, The everlasting Father, The Prince of Peace*' (2). The identity of the child is confirmed by the angel that visited Mary explaining that the babe she was to birth would, '*reign over the house of Jacob, and of His kingdom there shall be no end*' (3). Following this John the Baptist, Jesus Himself and His disciples heralded its arrival when they affirmed that the kingdom was, '*at hand*' (4). Then, after His resurrection, Jesus explained that '*all authority*' had been given to Him (5), and spent another 40 days explaining the workings of the kingdom to His disciples (6). This latter act makes very little sense unless of course the Kingdom was in operation at that time. The Psalms capture that in His ascension into heaven we are privy to the seat of His power when David writes, '*The LORD said unto my Lord, Sit thou at my right hand, until I make thine enemies thy footstool.*' (7). And just in case we missed its New Covenant

(1)Daniel 2:44; (2) Isaiah 9:6-7; (3) Luke 1:33; (4) Matthew 3:2; 4:17; 10:7; (5) Matthew 28:18; (6) Acts 1:3; (7) Psalm 110:1.

relevance, God repeats this fact five times later in Scripture (1). All of this is confirmed by Jesus' earlier comments that there would be some standing before Him who would not taste death, '*until they saw the Son of man coming in His kingdom*' (2). Now, if that were one or two vague Scriptures which could be misinterpreted perhaps there would be room to doubt its timing. However, Holy Spirit seems pretty determined we should understand that since its inception through Christ's death, resurrection and ascension the kingdom is here, and in operation, right now.

He brought us 'out'
That He might bring us 'in'
to the kingdom

Like the lady in Spurgeon's story above, I believe we have been blinded to our inheritance. Don't misunderstand me, there is no doubt that the cross IS the superlative door of entry! Unfortunately, many have come to that threshold and have camped there in the doorway instead of entering into that which has been opened to them. As a consequence the church may just have become irrelevant to a dying world, having been reduced to a historical society focused on the past - the baby in the manger, the cross, even Pentecost - rather than the pioneers of the '*greater things*' to which we were called. The theology of the cross is a 'must have' foundation, but the other side of the coin is that through our redemption we are also brought into a kingdom filled with the promises of God. This book is about seeing and entering that kingdom.

(1) Matthew 22:44; Mark 12:36; Luke 20:43; Hebrews 1:13; 10:12-13; (2) Matthew 16:28;

Our Parallel with the Exodus

The two-fold nature of our migration into the kingdom is found in Israel's exodus from Egypt. Here God spoke of bringing Israel '*out*' of Egypt that He might bring them '*in*' to the Promised Land (1). In hindsight it is evident that not all who came 'out' proceeded to go 'in'. I believe that Jesus was making a direct reference to this when He said to Nicodemus that it is one thing to '*see*' the kingdom and quite another to '*enter*' the kingdom you are seeing (2). In highlighting this progression - seeing to entering - to Nicodemus on the dawn of a new era He also made it applicable to us as New Testament believers. Of course, in speaking to Nicodemus *the teacher of Israel*' (3) in these terms He was referring to Moses and Israel, who saw but were unable to enter. These two stages of Israel's journey align with:

[1] Repenting, coming to the cross, recognising our sins are paid for in Christ who reconciled us to God, undergoing baptism and, secondly,

[2] Living in the promises of God, or in the language we have been using, moving into the kingdom (the Land of God's Promises).

While this would mean that the message of the cross is primarily for unbelievers, and the message of the kingdom for believers (notice, I said, '*primarily*'), it is vitally important to understand that the cross is not merely a 'one-time' experience. While a believer can say, they are saved because they have come to the cross, they cannot say, 'Been there, done that, bought the tee shirt', as though they were a tourist not wanting to revisit a

1) Deuteronomy 6:23; (2) John 3:3, 5; (3) John 3:10;

holiday destination. The Apostle Paul points out the ongoing and reciprocal nature of the cross when he says,

> 'Always carrying about in the body the dying of the Lord Jesus,
> that the life of Jesus also may be manifest in our body.'
>
> 2 Corinthians 4:10

To use a modern day analogy - and this falls miserably short - the cross is not solely the departure lounge for an unbelieving world, but is more like gaining an 'all day pass' that maintains access to all areas of the kingdom; a day pass that identifies not only the benefits, but also the ongoing cost to the wearer. Yes, that's right, there is a cost, because ultimately, the cross is not purely about the death of the Lord Jesus, it is also about our death! The cross is an ongoing yielding of one's life to the point where we, like the Apostle Paul, say,

> 'I have been crucified with Christ;
> it is no longer I who live, but Christ lives in me'.
>
> Galatians 2:20

Paul's confessions did not come overnight but should be attributed to an ongoing personal revelation that paralleled such yielding. For that reason, while this discussion chooses to focus on the kingdom, it will be found that Jesus and the cross are its centerpiece. An unveiling of the kingdom brings with it a commensurate revealing of the depth of the cross. However, our failure to recognize the two-fold nature of our redemption has given rise to a decided lack of teaching on the kingdom and hence its demonstration to a dying world. While the born again experience has been well documented throughout the years by theologians, there is relatively little revealing the kingdom. The main reason for this is that the kingdom requires us changing the current paradigm of our thinking. We have intellectually compartmentalised Scripture and theology, leaving a pronounced lack of material on the kingdom because it's a mystery to the carnal mind, in that it does not come intellectually or with outward observation, but enters through the door of our heart, delivered through revelation and accessed by faith.

---

*The two-fold nature of
Israel's exit and entry
parallels our own journey
more than we care to
acknowledge*

Without recognition that Christ's death opened the way into the kingdom of God we are in danger of being like Israel who, having left Egypt through the blood of the lamb and exited via the Red Sea, are now merely being sustained by manna in the wilderness (caught between two worlds), having heard of the Promises of God but not able to enter into experiencing them. God has deliberately demonstrated the two-phase nature of exit and entry in Israel's journey because it parallels our own more than we care to acknowledge.

Grapes, Pomegranates and Figs

Moses sent men to scout the Promised Land for 40 days to bring back news ahead of Israel's advance. They returned with a cluster of grapes from Eschol, pomegranates and figs. Such was the weight of the grapes that it required two men to carry them. As wine is made from grapes and wine is one of the metaphors for the Spirit of God the cluster carried by two men signifies a double anointing of God's Spirit. Because pomegranates are basically multiple seeds within a casing their inclusion alternatively with bells on the bottom or 'mouth' of the High Priest's garment speaks of the promises of God being decreed or 'ringing' out (1). Like the rest of the fruits that the scouts brought back, the meaning behind the figs may change with the context in which they are found. In this context I believe the figs signify 'peace and security', a meaning strongly associated with prosperous kingdom living (2). In summary, the fruits of the kingdom which they were to inherit were a double portion of God's Spirit, the promises of God, and peace and security. That supposedly random collection of elements just so happens to be what is on offer today as we transition from the church age to a kingdom one.

The Spirit Comes Out of the Water

Sometimes when you are looking at a scene you suddenly see the meaning behind it. Like when Jesus taught Nicodemus that to enter the kingdom one has to be born of the water and the Spirit or David faced Goliath. Both of these incidents parallel each

(1) cf. Luke 8:11; (2) 1 Kings 4:25; Micah 4:4; Zecharaiah 3:10.

other. For David the stone came out of a sling (a concave vessel and therefore picture of the heart), while for Nicodemus the Spirit comes out of the water. In other words, out of the well of His presence (including the written word within), comes the living word of revelation, carrying authority, direction or healing. That word becomes the catalyst for stepping into the kingdom. David's stone that hit its mark was representative of a word of revelation that changed the momentum of the battle in Israel's favor. Just as David was called to be king, you and I, too, are destined to rule. Just as he learned early to master the sling, we need to know how to source and use the revelation God gives us. The next chapter looks at the importance of revelation (God's living word of communication) as a foundation for entry into the kingdom.

SUMMARY

(1)There is noticeable lack of understanding of the two-fold nature of the cross.

(2)Jesus both atoned for our sin and gained entry for us into His kingdom

(3)The kingdom of God is here now.

(Acts 1:3 makes little sense if it isn't in operation now)

(4)There was a two-step process for Israel, God brought Israel 'out' that He might bring them 'in'.

(5)Israel's journey and struggle to enter parallels our own.

(6)The kingdom enters through the door of the heart, delivered by revelation and accessed by faith.

(7)Grapes, pomegranates and figs speak of the double portion of God's Spirit, proclaiming the word and being at peace and secure.

CHAPTER TWO

The Strength of Revelation

The other day I spotted a local church billboard that read, 'What will the kingdom of God be like?' Headlines like that stir me because it says the people are still wandering in the wilderness. Chances are they believe that someday this is suddenly all going to change overnight. They have been extradited from the world, but being blind to the kingdom they are disempowered to go forward. They don't understand that whilst we await a futuristic domain where the *child will play with the snake* (1), the kingdom is also here today. The man at the pool of Bethesda was similarly waiting for the stirring of the waters and for someone to help him get into its healing flow. He had been in that condition of impudence for 38 years, which is exactly the amount of time Israel were in Kadesh Barnea awaiting entry into Canaan. The two episodes parallel each other (2). Beneath the narrative that records this story is another of Israel powerless and waiting for a new messenger to come. In

1) Isaiah 11:8; (2) Deuteronomy 2:14; John 5:5.

saying, '*Arise take up your bed and walk*', Jesus who is The Message, didn't so much 'heal him', but rather moved him to realise what he already had. In regard to this incident, the human heart is at times envisioned as waters in Scripture (1), like the storm where Jesus came walking on the water. That scene was a precursor to the raging turmoil in the disciples' hearts after His death upon the cross. On the other hand, the impudent man's stirring waters are a picture of receiving revelation in the heart, awaiting the man of faith to stand and receive his healing.

Adjusting the Pendulum

After His resurrection Jesus taught the disciples for 40 days on the kingdom (2). It doesn't say He spent that time teaching about the cross, though as we will discover the cross did undergird all that He shared. If Jesus focuses on the kingdom after His resurrection perhaps we could justifiably spend more time doing the same. An adjustment to the pendulum of our teaching is needful so that we come to know as much about Jesus the Lion (King) as we know about Him as the Lamb (Suffering Servant). The main reason I believe we have camped at the foot of the cross and failed to go forward is because unlike 'the exit', which was God-initiated, the responsibility is upon us to 'enter'. And at this point, could it be, that like Israel, we also want to default to the security of the known because the opposition is formidable and entrenched. Once we understand that Israel's journey in the Old Testament parallels our own (3), key scriptures from the Old Testament provide us with much needed insight on our quest to enter the kingdom. One

(1) Proverbs 21:1, 18:4 & Matthew 12:34; (2) Acts 1:3; (3) 1 Corinthians 10:6,11.

such verse is found when Moses summarised the lessons of the wilderness. This is an opportunity for us to lean in and listen,

> *'And He humbled you, and suffered you to hunger,*
> *and fed you with manna, which you knew not,*
> *neither did your fathers know;*
> *that he might make you know that man*
> *does not live by bread alone,*
> *but man lives by every word that proceeds*
> *out of the mouth of the Lord.'*
>
> Deuteronomy 8:3

In summarising Israel's sojourn in the wilderness to the next generation why is this dependence on manna the thing that stands out above the rest and why would God want to teach Israel and the generations that followed this lesson? Looking at the verse, it is important to recognise that the life-giving manna is a metaphor for the word that *'proceeds'* from God's mouth. Thus, manna is a parallel of the 'rhema' or spoken word of revelation. Here the crux of the matter was that the wilderness experience of humbly looking to God for manna was to build within Israel the same critical need for revelation as they went forward. First up, the inclusion of past and present generations in not 'knowing' manna intimates that each successive age needs to recognize its own vital need of revelation. Also acknowledging that both current and past generations had never known manna suggests that this was more than just something new. If it was merely the introduction of something new it would have been sufficient to say that past generations hadn't known it. Of that generation that died in the wilderness we say with hindsight that they had a slave mentality which had them seeing themselves as *'grasshoppers'* in their own sight (1). The inclusion of the current generation (those not conditioned by Egypt) suggests then that this dependence on revelation presented more than a mere change to a limiting mindset based on past experience. It called for both deliverance from the past (limitations) and an equal challenge to the present (status quo). Therefore, what sets this lesson apart from all that Israel experienced in the wilderness was its emphasis on daily dependence on revelation.

Revelation alone provides the means to:

[1] Change limiting mindsets, and,
[2] Challenge any existing condition by providing the framework to go forward, creatively possessing the future before it becomes manifest.

Lastly, whereas it is possible to believe that the renewal of the mind is the attainment of a new level of understanding (2), the daily collection of manna says that it is to be driven by on-going revelation.

> *Revelation alone has the ability*
> *to challenge limited mindsets*
> *and provide a framework*
> *to move us forward*

---

(1) Numbers 13:33; (2) Romans 12:2.

Meditation: The Ground on which Revelation is Sown

Given this understanding, it should come as no surprise that the importance of revelation is reinforced on the very eve of entry into Canaan. When Joshua, as the earthly leader of Israel, was given his overarching instructions for taking the land (1), the center-piece of what was communicated was the importance of meditation day and night in the Law. Thus, following Moses' summation of wilderness lessons, comes a call to meditate on God's word because meditation is the fertile ground from which revelation flows. God said to Joshua,

'This book of the law shall not depart out of your mouth; but you shall meditate therein day and night, that you may observe to do according to all that is written therein: for then you shall make -- your way prosperous, and then you shall have good success.'

Joshua 1:8

This verse has an even stronger revelatory emphasis when considered beyond our limited English translations. On the surface, what is promised here is that by musing and chewing over the word of God (meditation), followed by obedience, one is guaranteed prosperity and success. Those two words in English have become something of a cliché. With greater specificity, the Hebrew word, *'prosperous'* here (Hebrew: Salah), is elsewhere translated as a 'rushing or breaking forth'. When you think about it, this is exactly what revelation is - a breaking forth of insight from another realm. Complimenting that is the Hebrew word

(1) Joshua 1:1-9.

here for *'success'* (Hebrew: Sakal), which also describes 'prudent understanding'. Thus, meditation in God's word promises revelation and the wisdom to know what to do with it.

Stepping Stones of Revelation

In the setting of what is recorded of Joshua's instructions this verse provides the hindsight necessary to appreciate an earlier promise God gave in the same passage, when He said, *'Every place that the sole of your foot shall tread upon I have given you'* (1). On one level Israel was assured possession of every acre of land into which they initiated a takeover. However, when we understand that the word, 'sole' is the Hebrew word 'Kaph' and that this describes a concave form such as a cupped hand, spoon or vessel, and that the human heart is also described as a concave vessel (2), we recognise a greater truth is being taught. When God deposits a spoken word or revelation in our heart, it becomes the ground on which we can put our weight in order to step into the kingdom. Similarly, when Peter stepped out on the water, he was not so much walking on water but upon the word spoken by Jesus to, *'Come'*.

Meditation begets Revelation, which begets Strength

When God gave Joshua instruction He went to great lengths to emphasise the need for strength. Three times in the same chapter and once in Deuteronomy (3) it is recorded that Joshua is to be, *'Strong and of good courage'*. The word, *'Strong'* is the Hebrew word, 'Chazaq' (חָזַק: Qoof, Zayin, Chet). Many Hebrew words convey

(1) Joshua 1:3; (2) Psalm 23:5; Acts 2:4; 2 Corinthians 4:7; (3) Deuteronomy 31:7.

their meaning pictorially. This word is a series of three pictograms ח: Chet (a wall), ז: Zayin (a weapon) and ק: Qoof (the back of a person's head). Together they spell out that strength is what follows breaking through a wall, ie strength follows receiving revelation. This passage as a whole reinforces for us that meditation begets revelation and revelation begets strength. In considering the other word accompanying 'Strength', we find the word 'Courage' is the Hebrew word, 'Amas' (אָמַץ) which is also made up of the three letters, Aleph (א: an ox head), Mem (מ: a body of water) and Tsade (ץ: a fishhook). The Ox is a symbol of strength, the body of water in between the other two letters pictures the human heart, while the fishhook means, 'Catch, need or desire'. These letters combine to spell 'Strong heart needed'. Thus, courage is the marshalling of one's heart around that which is strong (the revelation).

Revelation's Three-fold Strength

Before we leave this passage of rich instruction it is worth pointing out that the three verses calling Joshua to be strong and resolute each combine to provide a composite on the worth of the strength that comes from revelation. In the first instance, revelation strengthens him:

- To lead others to take possession of the inheritance (1).
- Next, he is strengthened to be obedient to, and not easily dissuaded from, the revelation given (2).
- And finally, he is strengthened to overcome fear, being assured of God's presence (3).

1) Joshua 1:6; (2) Joshua 1:7; (3) Joshua 1:9.

How important is revelation? From this passage it is evident that it guarantees possession of the promise, assures us of His presence to overcome fear, and girds our heart to follow through on what has been revealed.

The New Testament Need for Revelation

Having discussed references relating to Moses and Joshua's entry into the kingdom where is there New Testament evidence to support this theme of the importance of revelation?

That revelation is key to entry of the kingdom is shown in Jesus' use of parables to veil its treasures from unbelievers. The use of parables requires revelation to understand the truth behind the metaphoric scenes they present. Next, consider that the Book of Matthew, which focuses on Jesus the Lion (King) and His kingdom, presents its secrets clothed in Hebrew poetic form, where Holy Spirit *'teaches comparing spiritual things with spiritual'* (1). For example, the Beatitudes draw their truths from the Old Testament, requiring the hearer to be familiar with those passages from which they are drawn in order to enter the depth they present (2). Or, how about the occasions when Jesus spoke and people had no clue what He meant. His reference to *'sleep'* in regard to Lazarus, His conversation with Nicodemus, His apparent rebuttal of His mother at the wedding of Cana, all point to the fact that He was living on another level of reality. Most pointed in the light of our earlier discussion about manna is Jesus' directive on prayer where He bid us pray,

---

(1) 1 Corinthians 2:13b; (2) cf. Matthew 5:3 & Psalm 40:17; 5:4 & Psalm 119:136; 5:5 & Psalm 37; 5:6 & Psalm 42:1-2; 5:7 & Psalm 41:1; 5:8 & Psalm 24:3-4; 73:1; 5:9 & Psalm 133:1; 5:10 & Psalm 40

'Thy kingdom come.
Thy will be done in earth, as it is in heaven.
Give us this day our daily bread.'

Matthew 6:10-11

This is not, as has been regularly taught, a request for the means to earn daily provision. It couldn't be more to the point when we understand manna is revelation. This is an expectation that the kingdom will manifest here on earth when we ask for and receive manna (daily bread) from heaven.

Finally, there is the incident in the Book of Acts, where Jesus taught His disciples about the kingdom for 40 days after His resurrection, yet this teaching was not openly recorded. To discover what was taught requires revelation. All of this confirms that the kingdom is not of this world, it exists in another realm beyond the clutches of despotic men; a mystery deliberately hidden from the natural man so that it can only be accessed by believers exercising faith based on revelation.

If Joshua needed revelation
to lead God's people,
where are we taking them
without it?

Revelation and the Psalms

No discussion on revelation would be complete without a look at the opening to the Book of Psalms, where we read,

> *'But his delight is in the law of the Lord;*
> *and in his law does he meditate day and night.*
> *And he shall be like a tree planted by the rivers of water,*
> *that brings forth his fruit in his season;*
> *his leaf also shall not wither;*
> *and whatsoever he does shall prosper.'*

Psalm 1:2-3

The very first psalm primes its readers. It prepares them for the rest of the book by calling them to meditation because understanding of the realm of the poetic requires revelatory insight.

The use of a tree as a metaphor provides images that the heart can envisage, adding yet more facets to the worth and operation of revelation. In describing the product of meditation as the tree's life-giving water supply there is an immediate understanding that the roots or heart of man, rather than the head, is the avenue of supply. Reference to its fruit being seasonal reminds us that faith often requires tenacity and an appreciation of timing to see its reward. Leaves are often shaped like tongues and if they were to wither it would be a picture of words falling to the ground (1). Therefore, revelation also empowers us to speak or decree with authority (these are words that do not fall to the ground) to see

(1) cf. 1 Samuel 3:19.

'breakthrough' - which as seen earlier is the meaning of the word, 'prosper' that rounds off the verse. That authority accompanies revelation is also found hidden in the use of the word for meditate (Hebrew: *Hagah*) (1), when elsewhere it has been used to describes the roaring of a lion (2).

The Combined Importance of Revelation

Drawing from the lives of Moses and Joshua, with a little poetic input from the first Psalm, raises our awareness of the worth and importance of revelation as a catalyst for entry into the kingdom.

Revelation:

[1] Changes limited mindsets
[2] Challenges the status quo by providing the framework for possession of the promise (before it manifests)
[3] Strengthens the heart:
    (a) To lead others into their inheritance
    (b) To be obedient and not easily swayed
    (c) To overcome fear in the guarantee of His presence
[4] Provides a foundation for authority
[5] Is the vehicle for breakthrough

---

(1) Joshua 1:8; Psalm 1:2; (2) Isaiah 31:4.

Unearthing the Kingdom Throughout Scripture

Although Joshua and the Psalmist were restricted to the Law in their field of study, the reality for us is that this kingdom is found throughout the Bible. Revelation is actually the substance of the kingdom or, *'the treasure hidden in a field'* of Scripture (1). Every narrative, story and poetic verse contains glimpses of that other realm, albeit hidden and out of sight to the natural man. Once you get a taste of unearthing this 'lost' kingdom you will be forever hooked. There is a surface narrative, like the parables Jesus shared, and then there is the truth that lies beneath them. This is not to deny the value or veracity of the surface narratives. The Promised Land was metaphorically pictured as fruitful and flourishing by being described as, *'The land of milk and honey'* (2). As well as a summary of its bounty, this phrase also presents two boundaries to its depth: from milk to honey. Milk can be considered the surface story and the principles it contains, while honey is that which opens the eyes of understanding to deeper truths.

There is a surface narrative,
like the parables Jesus shared,
and then there is the truth
that lies beneath it.

Here's the amazing thing regarding the kingdom: rather than neglecting the cross, the main indicator to locating its treasures

(1) Matthew 13:44; (2) Exodus 3:8.

is discovery of the cross within the narratives, stories, poetic and prophetic passages throughout the whole scope of Scripture. So that, without the cross there is no kingdom.

Meditation: The Key to Making Revelation Your Reality

While this chapter focuses on the strength of revelation it needs to be said that revelation can, over time, become merely the gathering of more information. The key to continuing in revelation is found in meditation. One of the metaphors for believers is sheep. Sheep are animals classed as ruminants. Ruminants have four stomachs and derive and extract goodness from what they eat by chewing the cud'. That is, they regurgitate and 'chew over again' the food that they have already eaten. In this way further goodness is extracted after it has gone through a fermentation stage in the first stomach. Biblical meditation is based on this imagery of 'chewing over again' the word so that our heart can assimilate its nutrients. The key to imbibing revelatory teaching is taking time to meditate on each and every kingdom insight so that it is imbibed by our spirit. This is particularly true of areas that Holy Spirit highlights to you as you read, see or hear. Take your time when you are reading, not moving on to another subject until you have 'got it' and made it your own. Overlapping your study by reviewing previous material covered is also a useful tool to cementing it within.

SUMMARY

(1) We have camped at the foot of the cross because unlike the 'exit' which was God initiated, the onus is upon us to 'enter'.

(2) Israel's journey in the O.T. parallels our own.

(3) Deuteronomy 8:3 summarises the wilderness experience.

(4) Manna in the OT. parallels the rhema word of God.

(5) We need revelation (the rhema word) as they needed manna daily.

(6) Each successive generation needs to recognize its need for revelation.

(7) Revelation provides the means to:

(1) Change limiting mindsets

(2) Challenge existing conditions and provides the framework to creatively possess the future before it becomes manifest.

(8) The transformation of one's mind requires ongoing revelation.

(9) Meditation on God's word is the fertile ground from which revelation flows.

(10) Revelation provides spiritual strength.

(11) Meditation > Revelation > Strength

(12) Revelation strengthens by:

    (1) Guaranteeing possession of the promise

    (2) Assuring us of His presence

    (3) Girding our heart to follow through on what has been revealed.

(13) The N.T. call for daily bread is an expectation that the kingdom will manifest here on earth after we ask and receive manna from heaven.

(14) The lost kingdom is unearthed as 'treasure hidden in a field' of Scripture.

(15) Without the cross there is no kingdom.

(16) Discovery of the cross is an indicator to dig deeper in O.T. passages of Scripture.

(17) Just as sheep as ruminants 'chew over again' their food, so meditation is the key to imbibing and making revelation your reality.

CHAPTER THREE

A Kingdom of Sons

A Word of Caution

There are a number of things to be aware of when searching out layers in Scripture. Firstly, beware of a bias within yourself to get a passage of Scripture to say what you want it to say. If you are honest with a narrative it will generally expand and challenge the boundaries of your current understanding. For this reason, avoid rushing a passage. I will often spend weeks studying and meditating on an area to get it to yield its treasure. During this time I consciously choose to think and chew over what I have been working on: during worship, while driving my car, praying in tongues, lying in bed before I sleep, or listening to a sermon. I make sure I either record on my phone or note pad any thread of thought worth exploring.

Keep in mind that Bible chapter endings are not always correctly situated and be prepared to read beyond the neat chapter-limits of Western translators. For example, Isaiah chapter 53 starts in chapter 52:13; Genesis chapter one doesn't finish until chapter 2:3, John chapter 11 runs well into chapter 12. When I take notes I like to ask questions of Scripture, 'Why did he/she say that?' 'What is the opposite of what is taking place or being said?' Knowing that God likes to use personification and metaphor I ask, 'Who are the key players and who or what could they represent on another level?'

Next, recognise that a good spread of theological and Hebraic understanding is an advantage in seeing the landmarks that indicate where to dig and how to open a given passage. Finally, all that has been discussed here is built on the foundation of being born again (1) and having a dependence on the Spirit of God to lead (2).

Avoid Thinking 'Types and Shadows'

May I suggest as you read through this and other chapters on Christ in the Old Testament that you forget about 'types and shadows' but, instead, pursue the line of 'Aha, the kingdom revealed!' When we think 'types and shadows' we tend to expect a sketchy glimpse of Christ in the Old Testament. However, they reveal much more. These previews are not merely the warm up to the main event, they are multi-dimensional views of the greatest day in history. In the same way a holographic image is created by two or more projections, these insights provide an expanding 'whole-o-graphic' view (multi-layered and spiritually complete) of what was achieved through Christ. Together, they convey a

(1) John 3:3; (2) Romans 8:14.

greater depth than can be achieved by observing the events as they unfolded in the natural. Make no mistake, this is solid ground fought for and won by Christ to build on and inhabit.

The Whole of Creation is Awaiting

Everything we need to know about God's new kingdom is outlined in the Bible, except that it is hidden to natural eyes because kingdom living is living in the unseen realm, the faith realm. Jesus was alluding to this when He said, '*My kingdom is not of this world*' (1). Now, knowing that the seed-lot of faith is found in the book of Genesis, and the foundation of that book is its first chapter, you would expect to find pivotal nuggets of truth hidden within its veins. This is alluringly so when the Apostle Paul adds that, '*the creation eagerly awaits the revealing of the sons of God*' (2), and further to this that it is '*groaning*' in anticipation of our birthing (3).

The very first verse of Scripture says that, '*In the beginning God created the heavens and the earth*' (4). The following verses then unfold that creation. What I find interesting is that with an initial reading of these verses it appears that physical creation takes precedent. We read of the progressive introduction of light, earth, seas, plant life, sun, moon, fish, birds and land animals until finally man is presented as the climax of God's creation. However, the first verse seems to emphasise that the heavens, being mentioned before the earth, is foremost in God's plan. So is there a spiritual or heavenly truth we have not seen as we read rather cursorily through these verses? You be the judge as we unlock the spiritual

(1) John 18:36; (2) Romans 8:19; (3) Romans 8:22; (4) Genesis 1:1.

truths hidden here. Please understand I am not calling into question anything of the awesomeness of the physical creation, but rather simply looking at the majesty of our creator on another level. What I would like you to do as we proceed through this spiritual overlay of creation is to note when Jesus dies and is resurrected in reference to the creation week (on what days are these events depicted?) because like the first verse it reveals God's focus in the plan of redemption. First let us consider a basic outline of earthly creation, God:

1 Speaks light into existence and divides light from darkness.
2 Separates the waters above from waters below
3 Gathers the waters under the heavens and causes dry earth to appear. Plant life comes forth from the earth.
4 Sets the sun into the heavens to have dominion over the day,
Sets the moon and stars into the night sky to likewise have rule over the night.
5 Creates fish and birds to come forth from the seas.
6 Establishes land animals and then man, giving him dominion over all that has been created.
7 Rested from all that He created.

Now, let's reread those events looking at them through the lens of Scripture (1) so that we see them afresh.

Day One

On day one God revealed light to the world, which was shrouded in uncertainty, disorder and confusion (darkness) and emptiness (void). By introducing light He also separated and distinguished it from darkness. Spiritually this speaks of the

(1) 1 Corinthians 2:13b.

manifestation of Jesus to a darkened and disordered world, as it is He who is the light of the world (1). Like the introduction of light into darkness His introduction similarly divided and polarised people (2).

Day Two

Day two speaks of Jesus' death. How do we come to that conclusion? On every other day after He had created it is recorded that God saw that it was, '*good*'. However, on the second day God does not say it was good because the separation of the waters signifies the separation of Father (waters above) from Son (waters beneath). Death is the separation of waters. Thus when Moses led Israel through the Red Sea and when Elijah led Elisha through the Jordan each crossing symbolised passing through death. That the second day represents death is further reinforced as we come to day three.

Day Three

On the third day God gathered the waters under heaven into one place and then let dry land appear, then He imbued the earth to bring forth grass, herb that yields seed and fruit trees that bring forth fruit according to their kind, whose seed is in themselves. Unlike the second day - where there was no recognition of good - on the third day God saw that it was, '*good*', twice. The first recognition of goodness is because the earth coming out of

1) John 1:9-11; 3:19-20; 8:12; 9:5; 11:9-10; 12:46; (2) Matthew 10:34; John 7:12.

41

the waters symbolises the resurrection. How is that so? Well, in Scripture man is presented as an earthen vessel, Paul makes direct reference to this when he says, '*But we have this treasure in earthen vessels*' (1), a revelation that parallels Gideon having his men hide a flaming torch in an '*earthen*' vessel (2), which is linked to our origin in Adam as one drawn from the dust of the earth (3). Just as we baptise by full immersion, which depicts, death, burial and resurrection, the earth coming out of the water symbolises man's resurrection in Christ.

In recognition that men are as trees, spiritually, (4) God's second mention of goodness is tied to the inherent ability God has placed in this new creation (redeemed man) to produce fruit in accordance with the seed carried within. While it is tempting to deepen the discussion by unpacking this truth more, the purpose of this chapter is to present an overview that confirms our initial premise that God has invested more in the cross than redemption.

Day Four

Day four sees the establishment of the heavenly luminaries to divide day from night, the sun to rule the day and the moon and stars to have dominion over the night. Following the resurrection on the third day these events mirror the ascension of Christ who is now enthroned and seated in heaven (5). According to Malachi only those with faith can see it:

> '*But unto you that fear my name*
> *shall the Sun of righteousness arise with healing in His wings...*'
> Malachi 4:2

(1) 2 Corinthians 4:7; (2) Judges 7:16, 20; (3) Genesis 2:7; (4) Psalm 1:3; Jeremiah 17:5-8; Mark 8:24; (5) John 6:62; 20:17; Ephesians 1:20; 4:8-10; Psalm 68:18; cf. Isaiah 14:13.

Jesus the Son is also *'the Sun of righteousness'* and His victory in the cross and His following ascension marks the establishment of a new kingdom and His enthronement over it, where all authority has been given Him (1). The physical positioning of the Sun above earth and sky depicts His jurisdiction above heaven and earth. This speaks of His dominion over the roots of sickness in the spiritual realm and their earthly manifestations. The above verse also suggests that in His ascension Jesus, as *'the Sun of righteousness'* is healing more now than during His earthly ministry. Now that is food for thought! If we position our hearts to be irradiated in His glorious presence then this verse says He will overshadow us in healing.

As wonderful as that may be, it is not all that was set up on the fourth day. The moon and stars were also positioned to have dominion over the night. What is symbolised by this act is discovered when we look at this event in the light of other Scriptures. Firstly, as night is the absence of light this speaks of a time when Jesus is physically absent from the earth (2), as in 'now'. Then consider that when Jacob interpreted his son Joseph's dream of the sun, moon and eleven stars bowing down to him (3), he aligned the moon and stars as being his wife and sons (Joseph's brothers). Therefore the moon is a picture of his wife as she radiates his glory (3), just as we - the church (the Bride of Christ) - are called to radiate Christ's glory into a darkened world. This is in accordance with the fact that we spiritually have also been described as 'seated' (a place of authority) in heavenly places (4). The stars speak of us as Abraham's offspring (5). All the heavenly luminaries of day four are also said to be for *'signs'* and *'seasons'*, in Hebrew these

(1) Matthew 28:18; (2) John 9:5; 11:9-10; (3) Genesis 37:9-10; (4) cf. 1 Corinthians 11:7; (4) Ephesians 2:6; Colossians 3:1; (5) cf. Genesis 15:5 & Romans 4:13-16; Galatians 3:29.

two words speak of 'miracles' and 'appointed times' respectively. As sons and heirs of the kingdom we have been brought forth for such a time as this to spread the knowledge of the glory of God in the face of Jesus Christ as He works miracles through us.

Day Five

On the fifth day God spoke forth fish and sea creatures to populate the waters, and birds to grace the physical heavens. Both fish and birds can be considered to have wings. A fish or sea creature's fins and flippers are to it as wings are to birds, enabling it to soar and glide through the environment of water like a bird flies through the air. The two just live in different environments. Spiritually, winged creatures are spirit beings (1), and these two arenas are a depiction of the spirit realms above the earth and under the earth. How do I come to that conclusion you ask? In the same way that baptism parallels an earthly death, burial and resurrection. In the same way that Jonah's plunge beneath the waves reveal it to be a journey to, '*the belly of Sheol*' (2) and '*to the foundation of the mountains*' (3), where he recounted, '*The earth with its bars closed behind*' him forever. (3). Under water is under the earth, and in the sky is above the earth (4). The new covenant or kingdom significance of this day's creation is revealed in day six when God, having made man in His image, also gives him dominion over every area of His creation, which spiritually includes these two spirit realms (5).

(1) Isaiah 6:2; Hebrews 1:7; Revelation 14:6; (2) Jonah 2:2; (3) Jonah 2:6; (4) cf. Matthew 12:40; (5) Genesis 1:28.

Day Six

Before God made man on day six He made every land-based creature on the earth. Their description is both general and broad; they are simply listed as being cattle, beasts and creeping things. What is of interest to us is that though these literally describe animals of various species God also uses these names metaphorically at times to describe people, kingdoms and spirit beings. So we read of men described as creeping things (1), kingdoms represented as lions, bears and leopard-like creatures (2), and Jesus on the cross being surrounded by His earthly foes who are described as roaring bulls of Bashan who gape at Him like roaring lions (3). This latter scene can also be considered a picture of the spiritual forces using men as puppets arrayed against Him. Then, there is satan, who came to Eve as a serpent (4). Given everything that spiritually precedes this moment, it is apparent - having been made in God's image, and having been given dominion over His creation - that we, as sons of God, are to exercise a level of authority that we have generally ignored.

Day Seven

God blessed the seventh day and set it apart ('*sanctified*' it). It was not like all the other days. On all the preceding days the Bible records, '*evening and morning was the... day*'. On The seventh day there is no record of evening and morning. Notice that evening is the forerunner to morning because evening speaks of the death of Christ (Sun going down) and morning of His resurrection (Sun

(1) Habakkuk 1:14; (2) Daniel 7; (3) Psalm 22:12-13; (4) Genesis 3.

rising). This prophetic enactment took place six times (6 days) till everything was complete and in place so that God could position man in total rest. The place of rest was not reached after 3 days which signified Christ's resurrection. It was not complete even after the ascension depicted on the fourth day. No, God continued to add specific spheres of influence and authority so that the king's dominion (kingdom) encompassed every area and dimension. Nothing is outside its jurisdiction. Just as Boaz placed 6 measures of grain into Ruth's cloak (1) to telegraph the message that he would not 'rest' till her union and future was complete, so Christ has done the same here. Selah. The word 'sanctified' (Qadas: קָדַשׁ: Sheen, Dalet, Qoof) specifically used to describe the Sabbath spells out 'What follows the threshing'. Therefore, stopping at the cross effectively has us still on Boaz's threshing floor. Finally, the seventh day had no evening and morning because we now walk in the continuous light of an ever growing knowledge of the glory of God in the face of Jesus Christ (2). It is truly a New Day. Oh, how He deserves our praise!

Man Made in God's Image

The apparent culmination of His creation was the making of man in His own image. To fully appreciate the power and significance of this one act we will – in the next chapter - point out another facet outlined in the creation week. However, before we move on let's recap what has been outlined in this chapter. Beneath the description of the physical creation is the greater spiritual truth that the cross is the foundation of the establishment of the sons of God to rule and reign together with Him in His kingdom.

(1) Ruth 3:15-18; (2) 2 Corinthians 4:6; cf. Colossians 1:12; 1 Thessalonians 5:5; 1 John 2:8; Proverbs 4:18; 16:15.

A Spiritual Overlay of The Seven Days of Creation

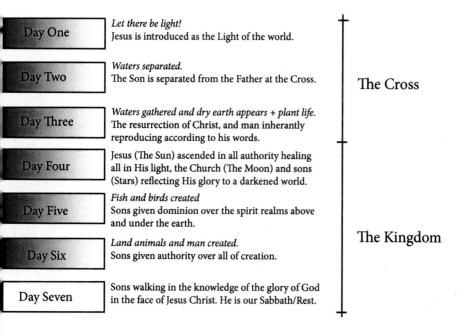

In unveiling the spiritual truth behind the physical creation, here is an even greater spiritual truth awaiting our discovery. Of the six days of creation the first three cover the manifestation, death and resurrection of Christ, leaving four further days to describe the inheritance His death has opened to us as sons. Where the church has been focused on God's exit strategy this chapter would suggest that God has always sought sons who would step through the cross to access a realm beyond these earthly constraints.

The victory of the cross and the establishment of His kingdom means:

- He has imbued man with creative abilities to be issued from his own mouth
- He has privileged sons to receive healing in His presence by faith
- He has seated sons in positions of authority.
- He has revealed His glory to sons that they may reflect it into a darkened world
- He called forth sons for such a time as this to see miracles
- He has given sons dominion over the spirit realms above and under the earth
- He has given sons rule over every physical and spiritual entity on earth.

SUMMARY

(1) Don't think 'types and shadows' when you see Christ in the O.T. think instead, 'Aha, the kingdom revealed!'

(2) Finding Christ in the O.T. provides a 'whole-o-graphic' view of what Christ achieved in the cross.

(3) Physical creation is summarised as:

    (1) Day One: The appearance of light and its division from darkness

    (2) Day Two: Water above and below separated

    (3) Day Three:

        (1) Waters under heaven gathered together.

        (2) Dry land appearing.

        (3) Plant life spring forth from the earth.

    (4) Day Four: Sun, moon and stars set in the heavens to have dominion over the day and night.

    (5) Day Five: Fish and birds created.

    (6) Day Six: Land and animals and man created, the latter to given dominion over all of creation.

    (7) Day Seven: God rested.

(4) The spiritual overlay of creation week:

    (1) Day One: Jesus introduced to a darkened world, His presence polarized people.

    (2) Day Two: He died and was separated from the Father.

    (3) Day Three: Jesus is resurrected, symbolized by the earth coming out of the water.

    (4) Day Four: The sun established in the heavens is the Sun of Righteousness arising with healing in His wings.

    (5) Day Four: The positioning of the moon and stars speaks of the lifting of sons, corporately and individually, at an appointed time to work miracles.

    (6) Day Five: Man given dominion above and under the earth.

    (7) Day Six: Man granted authority over all of creation.

    (8) Day Seven: Rest assured in the completeness of God's foresight and plan.

(5) Above all else the spiritual overlay of the creation week reveals that releasing sons into the kingdom was always His greater goal.

CHAPTER FOUR

Beyond Time

'A person starts to live when he can live outside himself.'
Albert Einstein

Having seen that the cross is not the end of the journey but that through revelation God wants us to enter in to His provision in and beyond the cross, we now turn to a facet of the creation week that is at the same time both exponentially exciting and challenging. It is evident that, like the disciples - who, after 40 days of teaching on the kingdom still asked when the nation of Israel would regain its former glory (1) - we too have difficulty renewing our minds to accept truth beyond our current grid of understanding.

═══════════════════════

(1) Acts 1:6.

Exploring Dimensions of Reality

In the twelfth century a Hebrew sage named Maimonides made a profound discovery when he asserted that God's creation is in ten dimensions. He made this discovery by observing the ten, '*and God said*' statements in Genesis Chapter One (1). More recently, Maimonides scriptural discovery of creation in ten dimensions has been confirmed by science (2). This means that our universe and existence as we know it, is now recognised by the world's leading physicists as being composed of more than length, width, depth and time - the four dimensions with which we are familiar. Particle accelerators, string theory and quantum mechanics have lead to ground-breaking findings, taking Einstein's theories of special and general relativity (which were themselves a leap forward, in incorporating time as a fourth dimension to 3D calculations) to yet another level. Spearheaded by physicists (3) and mathematicians (4) the scientific community has been led into recognising that a ten dimensional model best accommodates the previous inconsistencies which hindered a comprehensive theory of reality. Simply put, science has come up to speed, at least mathematically, to understand how a ten dimensional model best provides an integrated theory of our existence. Funny, that.

These relatively new findings of extra dimensions now provide a greater depth to better explain phenomena such as: Jesus walking through walls, the sun standing still for Joshua, the transportation of Elijah and Philip, and Jesus and Peter walking on water. The nature of these and other interactions between God

(1) Genesis 1:3,6,9,11,14,20,24,26,28,29; (2) *Beyond the Cosmos*, Hugh Ross PHD, Navpress, Colorado Springs, CO. ISBN 1-57683-112-4 (3) Schwartz *Beyond the Cosmos* p.36; (4) Witten & Seiberg *Beyond the Cosmos* p.37-38.

and mankind as set forth within Scripture show that He exists and operates both in and beyond the four dimensions which have defined and limited us.

It's exciting to realize that in this ten dimensional mix there must be multiple time dimensions or a super dimension that somehow incorporates time. This is suggested by a Creator who not only 'began' time as we know it by creating in 6 'days', Who speaks prophetically beyond each lifespan and Who is able to freely interact in time with His creation. With capacities like these it is little wonder that He appropriately calls Himself '*I Am*' and is found to be, '*the same yesterday, today and forever*'.

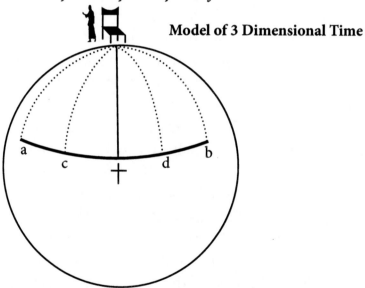

Model of 3 Dimensional Time

The line a - b represents the beginning and end of chronological earth time. With at least 3 dimensions of time God in heaven can interact with different individuals on earth from His throne in one instant of time. Alternatively, individuals 'c' and 'd' are equally able to access provision from the kingdom of heaven by faith from different epochs of time.

The Multiplication Miracles

This dimensional perspective beyond our own, helps explain such things as the multiplication miracles of Elijah and Elisha in the OT. This is where, for Elijah, a handful of flour in a barrel and a little oil in a jar did not stop giving throughout a drought; and for Elisha, where a jar of oil filled every empty vessel placed before it. It is interesting to note that each of these displays of 'endless' provision is followed by a 'resurrection of a son' (1). Previously these phenomenon had been thought of as previews of Christ before His earthly manifestation. They are, in fact, something much more revealing. These displays of a supernatural nature are demonstrations of the provision within the cross before its time. What we observe in each of these outpourings is a faith empowered cross-time-dimensional outburst of miracle provision. This is a display of New Testament (NT) truth BEFORE its time. Each is a preview of NT provision of drawing from heaven as later modelled by Jesus. The resurrections are not only confirmation of life beyond the 4D parameters in which we live, but they also act as a witness to the revival of the promises of God to the sons of God. Elijah and Elisha were simply moving as sons accessing heaven's storehouses by faith, BEFORE the cross had opened the door into eternity. OK, let's stop right there! One of our misconceptions about eternity (the realm beyond our own), is that it is outside time. Not so! Eternity is the 'fullness of time'. Every event that has and will ever happen is in eternity. Jesus came in the *fullness of time* not only in terms of our understanding of chronological time, but He also accessed and unlocked kingdom provision before its earth time.

(1) 1 Kings 17:8-24; 2 Kings 4:1-7, 18-34.

Let me explain. The beginning of miracles as recorded in John's Gospel takes place at the wedding of Cana where Jesus turns water into wine. In the lead up to that transformation Jesus' mother pulls on Him by saying, *'They have no wine'* (1). To which He responds,

> *'Woman, what does your concern have to do with Me?*
> *My hour has not yet come'*
>
> John 2:3

Current day Western thinking sees this response as offensive. However, Jesus is responding at a level different from immediate perception. In Jewish thought Jerusalem is a metaphor for the mother of the nation (2), and reference to a time they are to share in common is an Aramaic idiom for a future meeting. So that Jesus response is prophetic in nature. He is saying, in effect, *'I have a rendezvous with you [Jerusalem] (at the cross), when the wine of the Spirit will be poured out, but that time has not yet come.'* Therefore, when He goes ahead and performs the miracle He is accessing and demonstrating the provision of the cross before its time. Ultimately, He knew that as the incarnate word of God He was to be poured out that the joy of the Spirit may be experienced by all (water to wine/Word to Spirit).

Jesus again modelled the ability to transcend time when, for example, He forgave the woman caught in adultery because He did so based on the sacrifice He was yet to make (3). Similarly, He moved ahead of God's earthly agenda when He blessed the

1) John 2:2. (2) cf. Galatians 4:26; (3) John 8:3-11.

55

Syrophoenician woman before the dispensation of God's grace had been extended to the Gentiles. In both cases He bypassed chronological time and, by faith, harnessed heavenly provision before it had been unlocked. His miracles are a testament to the fact that from the time of His baptism Jesus lived as one dead because of His awaiting cross (1), ie He accessed heaven as one who was dead already. This aspect of drawing from heaven before its earthly time will be revisited later in this book.

Every anointing is associated with the death of the one receiving it

---

Some might say, 'What about Scriptures that say He was anointed to do the miracles' (2)? This verse endorses rather than discredits what is being said here it because an anointing is a declaration of a death. Every anointing is associated with the death of the one receiving it. I'm not talking only of Mary anointing Jesus in Bethany (3), but every anointing. Just as the separation of the waters represented the death of Christ on the second day of creation so kings were anointed not only to show they were chosen by God but also as a sign of the death of their personal life and separation to the purpose of leading the nation. Elisha was anointed at the Jordan (Jordan: means 'death' or 'descender') when he received the mantle fallen from his mentor and father, Elijah, after being separated out from the sons of the prophets (4). Priests were anointed as a sign of their consecration and separation into

(1) Isaiah 50:4-9; Luke 9:51; 12:50; (2) cf. Acts 10:38; (3) John 12:7; (4) 2 Kings 2.

their role of representing the people before God. Jesus was anointed at the Jordan when the Holy Spirit came upon Him, marking the end of His private life and the separation unto God for which He was called.

Created in God's Image

As we saw in the previous chapter God made man in His own image on the sixth day. There are various and endless theological discussions about what that looks like. Is man like God in being a spirit, or tripartite (body, soul, spirit), or creative, etc? I suggest that with our new appreciation of creation beyond chronological time (and recognizing that eternity is the fullness of time) that we may be able to dispense with theory. Outside of that chronological event in the eternal realm, Jesus the man already existed when God created man, so what if Jesus was the template God used!? Surely there is no other man more like God than Jesus? Son of God, Son of Man, the word become flesh. Therefore I'm suggesting that as Christ is the original template you are modelled on Jesus Himself. Now, that is certainly worth thinking through!

Back to the Future

This new dimensional perspective provides insights beyond our lineal perception of time, making us better placed to understand how God is not restricted by the limitation of an onward marching clock. Truths which were readied before the world began, and became hidden treasures within and without a chronological time-frame, are now able to be unlocked. In other words, much of what God wants to open up about New Testament essentials - the kingdom and the new creation - are found buried within the narratives of the Old Testament.

It is not uncommon to find that the reasons for apparent gaps in Scripture are often revealed elsewhere beyond the scenario we may be studying. The three year gap between Genesis Chapters 40 and 41 is not chronologically laid out, but is rather revealed in the butler and baker's dreams that preceded that period (1). Jesus victory on the earth, under the earth and above the earth, is not fully captured in one section of New Testament prose, but is parabolically laid out in the life of Samson (2). The depth of the gift of speaking in tongues is not plumbed in the four expressions of the gift set forth in the New Testament, but is found in the origins of the gift within the veil of the Old Testament (3). The steps to maturity that Jesus Himself took as a son are not progressively documented in the NT, but they are confirmed and outlined in His defeat of satan in the wilderness. I believe it is this dynamic of composite truth that Jesus was addressing when He referred to the scribe versed in the kingdom of heaven needing to bring out old and new to provide for his listeners.

Whilst it is possible to get
saved from one Scripture,
we will not grow without
exploring broader and deeper

---

(1) The Divinity Code to Understanding Your Dreams and Visions, Thompson & Beale, 2011, Destiny Image Publishers, P. 47ff; (2) *The Mystic Awakening*, Adrian Beale, Destiny Image Publishers, P. 129ff; (3) *The Mystic Awakening*, Adrian Beale, Destiny Image Publishers, P.111ff .(4) Matthew 13:52.

Whilst I believe that it is possible to be saved, in the grace of God, by accessing truth from as little as one verse of Scripture, we will not grow into maturity as sons of the kingdom without the depth and mix of nutrients provided by a meal of both preserved and fresh ingredients (4). The Old Testament prophets and Jesus' disciples were mentored for this very reason.

Leaven Hidden in 3 Measures

One of Jesus' parables compares the kingdom of heaven to leaven, which a woman took and hid in three measures of meal till the whole loaf was leavened (1). Many commentators see this as the corruption within the church because she also is referenced as a woman (2) and the act of 'hiding' the leaven is suggestive of deception. This imagery, and the demand for the omission of leaven from offerings due to its capacity to swell and corrupt, together with Jesus' likening it to the hypocritical teaching of the Pharisees (3) has given many commentators reason to color this parable in evil undertones. However, it needs to be noted that three measures of meal is recognised by the Jewish community as a fellowship offering, a meal over which guest and host communed together. This is drawn from Abraham's encounter with the Lord where he prepares a meal of fellowship and hospitality for his three visitors (4). Whilst there is legitimate grounds for a negative take on this parable, it needs to be noted that in explaining the leaven of the Pharisees Jesus says *'that there is nothing covered that shall not be revealed, neither hid, that shall not be made known'* (5). Putting aside our tendency to get locked into formulas, the use

1) Matthew 13:33; (2) Ephesians 5:25-32; (3) Luke 12:1; (4) Genesis 18:6. (5) Luke 12:2.

of leaven may simply refer to something '*hid that shall be made known*', which can have either positive or negative overtones. The three measures of meal could well be representative of Father, Son and Holy Spirit (symbolized by Abraham's three visitors), which in turn may be aligned with the Old Testament, Gospels and New Testament. Understanding Scripturally that Holy Spirit can also be metaphorically represented as a woman (1), opens our eyes yet further to another possibility that the Spirit who authored all Scripture (2) has deliberately hidden treasure in the three dispensations of Scripture - OT, Gospels, NT - so that in fellowship with Him their nuggets are unearthed to build up the Body of Christ into deeper communion with Him.

The Kingdom Masterclass

In the beginning of the Book of Acts Jesus is with His disciples for 40 days teaching them about the kingdom. This truly was His 'Kingdom Masterclass'. Yet, mysteriously, what He taught is not openly discussed in the passage. Here's the exciting thing: this is one of those hidden passages whose truth is revealed elsewhere in Scripture. I suggest that there is Scripture that details what He taught - and it's a passage that we are all familiar with - but we have not realized its deeper significance. In the next chapter we will open up this pre-cross teaching for you to judge for yourself whether it does in fact reveal the principles of the kingdom that Jesus taught His disciples in those 40 critical days of preparation before the coming of Holy Spirit. As we will discover, it is a pre-cross teaching that has huge post-resurrection ramifications.

(1) John 3:5; Romans 8:22-27; Genesis 8:6-12; Hebrew: 'Ruach'= 'Breath, Spirit' is female;
(2) 2 Timothy 3:16; 2 Peter 1:2

SUMMARY

(1) A ten dimensional model of reality best provides an integrated theory of our existence.

(2) God exists and operates beyond the 4 dimensions which have defined and limited us.

(3) Multiple time dimensions may best explain:

    (1) God's ability to speak beyond each lifespan

    (2) His name as 'I Am' and Jesus, who is, 'the same yesterday, today and forever'.

(4) The multiplication miracles can be accounted for by a multi-dimensional creation.

(5) The multiplication miracles in the OT are displays of provision within the cross before its time.

(6) Eternity is not outside time, it is the fullness of time.

(7) Jesus accessed heaven as one dead already.

(8) An anointing is a declaration of death.

(9) Christ is the original template you are modelled on.

(10) Much of what God wants to open up about the kingdom and new creation are buried in the narratives of the NT.

(11) To mature in the kingdom we require a mix of preserved and fresh ingredients.

(12) The Spirit of God has hidden treasure in 3 dispensations of Scripture -OT, Gospels, NT

(13) The Kingdom Masterclass is not openly discussed in Acts 1:3, but is found elsewhere in the NT where it is possibly the most profound pre-cross teaching with post resurrection ramifications.

OT = Old Testament; NT = New Testament.

CHAPTER FIVE

The Kingdom Masterclass

'These things all taken together Jesus said to the crowds in parables;
indeed, without a parable He said nothing to them.
This was in fulfilment of what was spoken by the prophet:
I will open My mouth in parables;
I will utter things that have been hidden
since the foundation of the world.'
Matthew 13:34-35

It is important to reiterate that whenever Jesus taught about the kingdom that He only did so using parables. Our understanding of the word, *'parable'* is limited and colored by our reading of the New Testament where the parables are seen as short stories told for a deeper spiritual meaning beyond the surface narrative. However, God has communicated in parabolic fashion throughout Scripture. The word *'parable'* has broader application than fictitious stories to illustrate truth. Parables are enigmas, riddles, mysterious sayings, proverbs. They include the enactments by the prophets, and even extend to the miracles Jesus performed, which can be considered parables in action. For example, Jesus spoke of the prophet Jonah being three days and three nights in the belly of the whale and then aligned Himself with that event by saying He would similarly be three days and three nights in heart of the earth (1). He then said that, *'a greater'* than Jonah was present (2). That *'greater'* was the parabolic message, hidden in Jonah, of the death and resurrection of Christ Himself. In modern terms, Jesus is both the script writer and true story on which Jonah is based. The creation account as was discussed earlier is yet another example of the treasures of the kingdom hidden parabolically in an Old Testament narrative.

Why does He use parables to communicate the kingdom? Jesus used and is still using parables because they have a multifold purpose, they:

[1] Fulfil the word of Isaiah (Isaiah 6:9-10)
[2] Shield the kingdom from unbelievers (Matthew 13:11)
[3] Relate and frame heavenly things in earthly language to believers
[4] Stop despotic people from misusing the kingdom
[5]Anchor and make memorable kingdom truths
[6] Require a knowledge and relationship with God
[7] Are part of the maturing process - the language of the Spirit
(the milk to meat journey)
[8] Bypass our inner defence mechanisms - eg David/ Bathsheba
(2 Samuel 12:1-7)

---

(1) Matthew 12:40; (2) Matthew 12:41.

That God speaks parabolically about the kingdom is sadly overlooked by many today. As a consequence many are ignorant of the layers in the Scriptures that reveal deeper parabolic truth. It is possible that many church-splits, building problems, acts of fornication and adultery could have been avoided - or their collateral damage minimised - had someone understood the parabolic nature of the voice of the Spirit and foreseen what was happening.

The Geography

Before we jump in to reveal what I believe to be the most overlooked passage of Jesus' teaching, it would do well to understand what is conveyed in the geographical setting in which it is delivered. Consider the account of Moses going up the mountain with God to receive instructions on the construction and furnishing of the Tabernacle. The New Testament equates the encounter as an audience before God in heaven (1). Therefore, climbing the mount parallels entry into heaven (2).

The Kingdom Masterclass

It will become evident that the passage of Scripture in question is more than a random teaching and that the heading which has traditionally been assigned to it causes our perception of this material to fall way short of its true worth. We need to recognise that the habit of publishers ascribing headings to sections of Scripture is both a benefit and a hindrance. Yes, headings help

1) Hebrews 8:5; (2) cf. Psalms 107:26; Hebrew 12:22.

65

us locate passages more readily, but they also condition the reader to preconceived ideas and put 'blinders' on what they see. To go beneath a surface reading of Scripture and extract the treasure to be found, the reader needs to ignore these superficial headings. With that brief introduction, I suggest that the material Jesus expounded in Acts chapter 1 was what we have come to know as 'The Sermon on the Mount' (TSOTM). Let me expound the evidence for this assertion.

'For theirs is the kingdom of heaven'

What initially earmarks the beginning of this passage for further investigation is the repeated use of the phrase, *'for theirs is the kingdom of heaven'* which is found in the first and last of the Beatitudes. This signpost is part of a Hebrew poetic form, known as an inversion or chiasm, which in this case acts to highlight and seal the Beatitudes' subject matter:

Blessed are the poor in spirit: **for theirs is the kingdom of heaven.**
   Blessed are they that mourn...
      Blessed are the meek...
         Blessed are they which do hunger and thirst for righteousness...
      Blessed are the merciful...
      Blessed are the pure in heart...
   Blessed are the peacemakers...
Blessed are they which are persecuted... **for theirs is the kingdom of heaven.**

Matthew 5:3-10

The Word 'Blessed'

Jesus use of the word, '*Blessed*' to open each of the Beatitudes (1) is incredibly significant. I used to believe that this word was based on the Hebrew, 'Barack', which means to kneel and receive a blessing from a superior. Much has been written by others about the power and importance of this type of blessing. However, in Matthew this is not the root of the word used. The word '*Blessed*' (Greek: Makarios) in operation here, comes from the Hebrew word, 'Asher' which means, 'Happy'. Here is the interesting thing about this word. In Hebrew, the word, Happy (Asher) is made up of the letters, Aleph, Sheen, and Reysh (אָשֵׁר). Aleph(א) and Sheen(שׁ) together spell out, 'Strong Devourer'. A combination that elsewhere is frequently interpreted as 'Fire'. 'Reysh'(ר) is the Hebrew letter that means 'Head'. Therefore, the word, '*Blessed*' literally can be translated as 'Fire on the head'. Just stop and think about that for a moment in the light of what took place on the Day of Pentecost. The repeated use of this word in preparation for what was to follow is astounding!

The Mountain

Now that a beachhead has been established let's go further and gain territory beyond the front lines. There are two main points to be grasped in the introduction to this passage. First and foremost is the setting on which the teaching takes place. Here we are told that, '*And seeing the multitudes, He went up a mountain*' (2). Simple, yet profound. So simple in fact, that without our

(1) Matthew 5:3-10; (2) Matthew 5:1.

introduction we could easily miss it. How many times have we skipped over those words not realising their worth? Jesus is, in type, ascending into heaven. This is emphasised, in the Greek, where we read that it was not merely '*a*' mountain, but rather, '*THE*' mountain (1). And it is to this place that His disciples, not the masses, come to Him. Can I suggest that - combined with the evidence that the passage is yet to yield – this physical mountain is meant to correlate with entry into heaven? What I am saying is that once Jesus took His heavenly throne that it was there that His disciplined ones come to Him and it was there that He taught them (2). What this means is that the event of Jesus climbing the mount that day - and the way it is recorded - is parabolic in nature. In other words, the main event, namely His entry to heaven, is depicted here veiled in parable. Coming back to this passage, note that the journey 'upward' was precipitated by Jesus seeing the '*multitude*', which is echoed elsewhere in John's Gospel when Greeks (the rest of the world) seek an audience with Him, to which He responds, '*The hour has come, that the Son of Man should be glorified*' (3). Clearly, the world's awakening desire for an audience with Him is the signal that it is time to establish His greater kingdom.

Depth of Teaching

Next, it is important to acknowledge that the Sermon on the Mount sets forth such detailed teaching that it would be impossible to plumb its depths in a cursory reading or Sunday sermon. The nature of how these truths are set out and then unfolded demands time spent to ensure their understanding and

(1) Greek; 'To Oros' ='The mountain'; (2) cf. John 20:17; (3) John 12:20-23.

absorption. Is it possible that Matthew, the accountant, is able to record this incredible passage with such detail because it was revisited by Christ in different settings in the other gospels and then repeatedly between His resurrection and Ascension? Weighing in on this argument is the fact that Matthew himself does not join Jesus' party of followers until Matthew 9:9, yet his coverage of the Sermon on the Mount is remarkably comprehensive.

The Sermon on the Mount
is a pre-cross teaching
bearing
post-resurrection secrets

The Outline

Like the establishment of its predecessor in the Book of Exodus, where the Ten Commandments provide a base, this new kingdom covenant presents a set of precepts that are progressively expanded. In outline, Jesus sets forth the Beatitudes, the Sermon on the Mount expands on and applies these precepts, and the rest of Book of Matthew is then both a reiteration of the truths they contain and a demonstration of them in operation. Also like its predecessor, the Book of Matthew sets forth 8 woes which Jesus pronounced over the Pharisees to seal, confirm and close this kingdom teaching. These are the antithesis of the 8 blessings contained in the Beatitudes. The blessings of the Beatitudes and the woes spoken over the Pharisees bookend the Kingdom that is revealed in Matthew's Gospel (see overleaf).

Blessings vs Woes (1)

Blessings	Woes
Matthew 5:3-10	Matthew 23:13-36
1. Poor in spirit have kingdom opened to them	1. Proud in spirit shut the kingdom to others
2. Mourners comforted	2. Mourners pillaged
3. Meek inherit earth	3. Zealous hypocrites inherit Gehenna
4. Heart righteousness satisfied	4. Superficial righteousness confirms blind leadership
5. Merciful obtain mercy	5. Mercy neglected
6. Singleness of heart causing vision	6. Duplicity of heart causing blindness
7. Union with God begets His likeness	7. Hypocrisy and lawlessness declare His absence
8. Persecuted for righteousness are endorsed	8. Persecutors of righteousness condemned

Matthew's Gospel
(The Gospel of the Kingdom)

Prologue 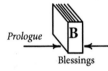 *The Kingdom* *Epilogue*

Blessings   Woes

The Kingdom's
Structural Base

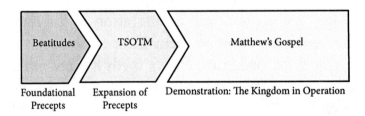

Beatitudes   TSOTM   Matthew's Gospel

Foundational   Expansion of   Demonstration: The Kingdom in Operation
Precepts   Precepts

(1) cf. Deuteronomy 28 (Blessings and Cursings). TSOTM = The Sermon on the Mount.

Forty Days

The challenging nature of the material Jesus introduced into the disciples misconceptions of the Kingdom is in keeping with Jesus taking 40 days to unfold it. The depth of the material aside for a moment, why does the Book of Acts record that He was with the disciples 40 days teaching about the kingdom? Why was Israel 40 years in the wilderness? Why did Noah's flood culminate after 40 days and nights of rain? Why did Goliath present himself to Israel for 40 days and 40 nights? Why was Jesus 40 days in the wilderness? Why did He mentor His disciples for 40 Months (3 1/2 years minus 40 days in wilderness)? The reason the number forty is chosen is because it conveys, 'Gestation', and in particular, 'Gestation of a New Creation'. Jesus imparted the principles of the kingdom to His disciples so that once they were empowered by Holy Spirit they would understand how to operate as new creations in the kingdom.

Foundational Teaching

The critical importance of this foundational teaching is not only witnessed by the fact that some of it is repeated in Luke's Gospel in a teaching that takes place on a plain, but even more so in the closing remarks in the Sermon on the Mount. This is where Jesus magnifies the vital nature of its application. He says, *'He who does these sayings...will build his house on a rock'* (ie a solid foundation), and he who does not do them will be built on sand (1).

1) Matthew 7:24-27.

Pre-Cross Teaching with Post Resurrection Application

To close this chapter, let us consider other new covenant treasures from TSOTM that confirm that Jesus was presenting a pre-cross teaching with post-resurrection application. These are realities that most certainly only apply after His death and resurrection. The first of these is found in His statement,

'You are the light of the world... Let your light so shine before men, that they may see your good works, and glorify your Father which is in heaven'

Matthew 5:14-16

Outside of this passage, Jesus continually emphasises that He is the Light of the world (1), and yet here He asserts that His disciples are the light of the world. That believers are lights in the world is a truth only disclosed after the resurrection by the Apostle Paul (2). How could Jesus' words be true unless He was talking of a truth yet to be realised. When Jesus initially taught the Sermon on the Mount, His glory was not yet housed in believers. Our privilege - as light bearers - awaited our cleansing through His death upon the cross.

On another front, the second of the eight precepts Jesus taught is, *'Blessed are those that mourn for they shall be comforted'* (3). While mourning and fasting are not mutually dependent, it is very common for people not to eat when their hearts are deeply affected by the absence of a loved one. In teaching the disciples

(1) John 8:12; 9:5; 11:9; 12:46; (2) Philippians 2:15; (3) Matthew 5:4.

of John the Baptist, Jesus not only provided an association between mourning and fasting that our generation seems to have overlooked, but also explained that the latter is inappropriate while He is still with them. When Jesus is no longer physically present then His disciples will mourn His presence and internally declare their desire for Him by fasting. Is it possible that Jesus taught a foundational principle here that only has application after His ascension?

'Then came to him the disciples of John, saying, Why do we and the Pharisees fast oft, but thy disciples fast not?
And Jesus said unto them, Can the children of the bridechamber MOURN, as long as the bridegroom is with them? but the days will come, when the bridegroom shall be taken from them, and then shall they FAST...
Neither do men put new wine into old bottles: else the bottles break, and the wine runneth out, and the bottles perish: but they put new wine into new bottles, and both are preserved.'

Matthew 9:14-18

There is a very strong suggestion that this second Beatitude and His later teaching to the disciples are linked in the mourners being 'comforted' (1). Who is it that comforts? Who else, but The Comforter (2). It's not surprising then that the 'comfort' delivered to those who mourn is also expressed in the verses above as coming in the form of new wine, after the vessels have been changed. Having believed, fasting not only communicates the earnestness of our desire for Him, it also crucifies the flesh in preparation for

(1) Matthew 5:4; (2) John 14:16, 26; 15:26; 16:7.

73

a fresh infilling of His Spirit. Could it also be that the foundational role of fasting in the kingdom is largely overlooked today? Jesus reinforcement of *'when'* not *'if'*, you fast, would suggest He expected it (1). With this understanding, we can appreciate that the disciples would have applied fasting with their prayers and supplication as they awaited power from on high (2).

Could it be that the
foundational role of fasting
in the kingdom is largely
overlooked today?

It should be evident that Jesus' Sermon on the Mount is much more than just another Sunday sermon, to be replaced by a different topic the following week. The weight of evidence is tipping the scales to its great kingdom relevance today:

In review:

[1] By the fire on the heads at Pentecost
[2] not 'a' mountain, but *'The'* Mountain
[3] Recognizing the setting - being seated, disciples coming to Him.
[4] The action taken of climbing the mountain on seeing the multitudes
[5] The depth and documentation of the subject matter
[6] Its contrast and closure with the 8 woes (bookends)
[7] The 40 days of gestation of a new creation
[8] Jesus declaration of its foundational importance
[9] Pre-cross teaching having post-resurrection application:
      (a) You are the light of the world (3)
      (b) Blessed are those that mourn (4)

(1) Matthew 6:16; (2) Acts 1:14; (3) cf. John 8:12; 9:5; (4) cf. Matthew 9:14-18.

Whatever your verdict, I'm sure you would agree that the Sermon on the Mount deserves a deeper archaeological dig by kingdom seekers. I'm sure some of you are ahead of me because there are a multitude of questions both raised and answered in Jesus' post-resurrection instructions on the kingdom. My goal in writing this book is not to write a commentary on the Book of Matthew but to challenge our mindsets and stir us into purposeful exploration of the kingdom into which we have been translated. The next two chapters draw further on often overlooked truth from Matthew's treasure chest of kingdom gems as we move on.

SUMMARY

(1) Jesus used a parable every time He taught on the kingdom.

(2) Parables are found throughout Scripture, they include:

(1) Enactments of the prophets.

(2) The miracles Jesus performed - parables in action.

(3) Parables have a multi-fold purpose.

(4) Layers in Scripture also reveal deeper parabolic truth.

(5) Symbolically, climbing a mountain parallels entering heaven.

(6) TSOTM is the Kingdom Masterclass.

(7) The Hebrew root of word 'Blessed' as used in the Beatitudes means, 'Fire on the head'.

(8) The TSOTM was delivered on 'The Mountain'.

(9) The depth of teaching of TSOTM requires time to digest it.

(10) The Beatitude set forth the precepts of the kingdom, the TSOTM expands them, and the Gospel demonstrates them in action.

(11) There are 8 woes in Matthew 23 that are the antithesis of the Beatitudes. Together they are the bookends of the kingdom revealed in Matthew.

(12) 40 represents the 'Gestation of a new creation'.

(13) TSOTM is foundational kingdom teaching because Jesus defined its doers as those built on a rock.

(14) Confirming TSOTM is a pre-cross teaching with post resurrection application is:

(1) 'You are the light of the world'

(2) Blessed are those that mourn because it relates to those fasting after His departure.

CHAPTER SIX

The Presence of God

Charles Finney (1792-1875) was an American Presbyterian preacher known for his revival services and extemporaneous preaching. There were times in Finney's life when the presence of God was so tangible that people were brought to repentance without a word being spoken. He recounts the story of when he was called to preach at a manufacturing village. The next day he was invited to tour the manufacturing operation at a local factory. On entering the weaving department he saw lots of young women, some of whom looked at him, and then at each other, in a way that indicated they were distressed, and that they knew him. Finney knew none of them. As he got nearer to them their agitation increased. He stopped and looked at them and as he did one of their number broke a thread and could not fix the problem because her hands were trembling too much. As he continued to observe the group, the trembling spread to the other women until they left their looms and fell on their knees to the floor in lamentation. Finney had said nothing, and even if he had the noise of the looms would have smothered it, but the presence he carried convicted each worker without a word.

There is a universal presence of God and a manifest or tangible presence of God. What Finney carried was the manifest presence of God. Adam and Eve hid, and Jonah ran, from the manifest presence of God. On the other hand, the prophet Jeremiah was talking of the universal presence of God, when he penned,

'Can any hide himself in secret places that I shall not see him?
says the Lord.
Do not I fill heaven and earth? says the Lord.'
Jeremiah 23:24

Just about everybody knows that the God professed by Jew and Christian alike, is meant to be everywhere at the same time, ie that He is omnipresent. What they do not know is that there is a manifest presence of God that is promised to accompany believers. Many may have experienced His presence in a corporate setting as the congregation expresses its desire for Him in worship, but individually we also have the privilege of hosting the presence of God. Such is the distinction and contrast of those who host His presence that Samson was led to say he would become, *'weak and be like any other man'* without Him (1). Moses said it was the manifest presence of God that separated the Israelites from all the other people on the face of the earth (2). He also acknowledged

(1) Judges 16:17, 20; (2) Exodus 33:16.

78

how precious the manifest presence was to him when he said that he didn't want to go up into Canaan without Him. In response, God promised Moses that His *'Presence will go with you and I will give you rest'* (1). When Jesus stepped into the boat full of disciples struggling at the oars because the wind was contrary the Bible records that *'immediately they were at the land where they were going'* (2). The Book of Psalms prefigures that day by saying,

'He makes the storm a calm, so that the waves thereof are still.
Then are they glad because they be quiet;
so he brings them unto their desired haven.'
Psalm 107:29-30

When Jesus stepped into the boat they were immediately at their desired haven (a place of rest). His joining them was a prophetic foretelling of the fulfilment of God's word to Israel that He would go with them and bring them rest. His presence was their ultimate rest. For Israel's kings the Promised Land occasionally had rest from their enemies (3). The Book of Hebrews in making reference to this fact, follows by explaining that the physical entry into Canaan still awaited a promised rest for the people of God (4). And prior to Jesus stepping into the boat the disciples thought they had seen a spirit (5). They did so because Jesus in our midst, as Holy Spirit, is our rest.

Coming back to Matthew's gospel, we have already discussed that the Beatitudes laid the foundations for the kingdom. We have also seen that leading each of these eight Scriptures is the word,

---

(1) Exodus 33:14; (2) John 6:21; (3) 2 Samuel 7:1; (4) Hebrews 4:8-9; (5) Matthew 14:26.

'*Blessed*', which, whilst a Greek word (Makarios), comes from the Hebrew word, Asher. In Hebrew, Asher (אָשֵׁר) is made up of the letters, (אָ)Aleph, (שֵׁ) Sheen, (ר)Reysh, which spells out 'Strong devourer on the head' or more precisely, 'Fire on the head'. It's here that the Beatitudes link with our current subject of the presence of God because fire on the head is symbolic of the presence of God. So each of the Beatitudes could be read as,

The presence of God is with the poor in spirit...
The presence of God is with those that mourn...
The presence of God is with the meek...
The presence of God is with those who hunger and thirst for righteousness...
The presence of God is with the merciful...
The presence of God is with the pure in heart...
The presence of God is with the peacemakers...
The presence of God is with those who are persecuted...

The Beatitudes lay the foundation of the kingdom in guiding us to become carriers of His presence because the presence of God is the kingdom!

The Hebrew word, 'Asher'
or 'Blessed' in its original form
depicts 'Fire on the head'
which signifies
the Presence of God!

The Presence of God is the Kingdom

In terms of proof that the Beatitudes are pre-cross teaching with post-resurrection application 'the fire on the head' not only presents a link to Acts Chapter 2 (as pointed out earlier), but is also reference to a time when Israel was poised to enter the Promised Land. At that time Moses was reasoning with the Lord about not giving up on His people. He described Israel through the eyes of the nations around them, by stating,

'...for they have heard that You Lord are among this people,
that You Lord are seen face to face,
and that Your cloud stands over them,
and that You go before them, by day time in a pillar of a cloud,
and in a pillar of fire by night.'

Numbers 14:14

Allow me to draw a parallel here. God's glory was over Israel and was seen in the cloud by day, by those who looked on. Likewise, in fulfilling all that was written about Him (1) Jesus ministered while it was day (2) and manifested His glory (3) to those who had eyes to see. As the true light of the world (4), Jesus' presence represented the day, and His pending physical departure represented the night - a time when His glorious presence would be seen as a pillar of fire over His people. In preparation for the night, Jesus laid down the foundations of the kingdom in the set of Scriptures that depict the presence of God as fire on the heads of His people. Like Moses before Him, Jesus stood poised on

(1) Matthew 5:17; (2) John 9:4; (3) John 2:11; (4) John 8:12.

the doorstep of the kingdom and described what would set His followers apart from the world around them: namely, the presence of God.

The Promised Land

The word, *'earth'* in both Hebrew and Greek may legitimately be translated *'land'* (1). When Scripture says we *'have this treasure in earthen vessels'* (2), and Gideon's men hid torches within earthen pitchers (3); that the sons of Zion are as the work of the potter (4) and that we are an earthly house (5), we also may be considered to be *'land'*. Which means, where for Israel the kingdom was the physical Promised Land, for us it has become 'The land of God's Promises in us'. This reinforces that we are bearers of the kingdom, and suggests that the extent of its boundaries reach only as far as we have built on the revelation of His word. This does not in any way negate Israel's right to the physical land.

Its the tangible presence of God
that sets believers apart
from every other person
on the planet

Now, in the light of our discussions on the kingdom and our current understanding of its link to His presence, we can understand more fully why Jesus would say,

'He who abides in Me, and I in him, bears much fruit;
for without Me you can do nothing' .

John 15:5

(1) cf. Psalm 37:9 & 37:29; Matthew 5;5 & 13:5; (2) 2 Corinthians 4:7; (3) Judges 7:16-20; (4) Lamentations 4:2; (5) 1 Corinthians 5:1.

His presence is everything to us. Indeed, without it we are the same as everybody else on the planet, incapable of the supernatural; but with it we are His new creation filled with potential to manifest the kingdom. The Bible attributes a multitude of benefits to His presence: angels accompany His presence (1); the enemy is defeated in His presence (2); we are hidden and protected in His presence (3); and His presence supplies a fullness of joy and provision,

> '*In Your presence is fullness of joy;*
> *at Your right hand are pleasures for evermore.*'
>
> Psalm 16:11

There are two facets to what is meant by being at the '*right hand*' here. Firstly, consider that the sheep were separated to the right and the goats to the left (4) and the disciples were to throw the net out on the right side of the boat (5) because the right side represents the exercise of faith. Next, the right hand speaks of the hand of fellowship (6). This suggests that when Jesus fed the 5000, when the bin of flour and the jar of oil did not run out (7), when Elisha filled all the empty vessels with oil from a single jar (8), that they all did so fellowshipping in the presence of God by exercising faith (9).

---

1) Psalm 63:9; Luke 1:19; (2) Psalm 9:3; 68:2; 97:5; (3) Psalm 31:20. (4) Matthew 25:32-33; 5) John 21:6; (6) Galatians 2:9; (7) 1 Kings 17:11-16; (8) 2 Kings 4:2-7; (9) cf. 1 Kings 17:1; Kings 3:14; Matthew 14:19.

SUMMARY

(1) There is a universal presence of God and a manifest presence of God.

(2) It is the manifest presence of God that separates us from other people.

(3) Jesus in our midst as Holy Spirit is our rest.

(4) The word, 'Blessed' (Hbw: Asher) means 'Fire on the head' which signifies the presence of God.

(5) His presence is the kingdom, that's why when He stepped into the boat they were there.

(6) The cloud by day and fire by night continued in NT with Jesus ministry and now His presence.

(7) The Promised Land is now the promises of God in us (this doesn't negate Israel's right to the land).

(8) 'In your presence is fullness of joy, at Your right hand there are pleasures forever more.'

The right hand speaks of the hand of faith and fellowship.

CHAPTER SEVEN

Two Kinds of Righteousness

Overt and Covert Division

The opening stratagem of chess is the early positioning and occupation of one's forces exerted through the center of the board. With this in mind the most common first move is a king's pawn thrust into the void between the two armies. What follows is an attempt to progressively strengthen and support that position before more offensive moves are made. This is because whoever controls the center commands the battlefield and effectively divides, hampers and restricts the opponent's pieces. Reinforcing this is an adage touted by chess buffs, 'A knight on the rim is dim'. Whether we are considering two kingdoms seeking to exert dominion on a chessboard or spiritual forces arrayed in the heavens, the principle is the same: if you can divide you can conquer. Israel applied this axiom by targeting and gaining the victory at Jericho, effectively dividing the sum total of Canaanite forces that could be arrayed against them. However, what happens openly on the battlefield may also be applied behind the lines, both individually and corporately, amongst members of a squadron, team or side. Jesus addressed that issue when He said,

'*...every kingdom divided against itself is brought to desolation; and every city or house divided against itself shall not stand.*'
Matthew 12:25

Division is both the most overt and covert of spiritual strategies. Like David hurling the right stone at the precise time to hit the mark in Goliath's skull, we are on the offensive when we decree and declare the rhema (quickened) word of God to split open the forces arrayed against us. But we become victims when:

[1] we listen to word seeds of doubt and fear that divide the unity between our head and heart;
[2] we give the flesh authority over our spirit by criticising our colleagues;
[3] busy-ness distracts us from hearing and inculcating revelation truth (failing to imbibe the word) so that it can become one with us.

The Kingdom and Unity

Why is this so important? Because unity plays a pivotal role in hosting the presence of God. It is no wonder the devil seeks to divide us; he knows the threat our unity is to his kingdom. Jesus laid it out like this,

'... *if two of you shall agree on earth as touching anything*
that they shall ask,
it shall be done for them of My Father which is in heaven.'
Matthew 18:19

First, He promised there would be fruit from focused spiritual alignment and then qualified the foundation from which it would come by saying,

'*For where two or three are gathered together in My name,*
there I am in the midst of them.'
Matthew 18:20

Without question: where the King is there is also the kingdom with all its glorious provision.

Where the King is
there is the kingdom
with all its glorious provision

Unity is such a critically important factor to our effectiveness in the kingdom that Jesus spent a good part of His Masterclass expounding the subtleties of personal division (1). This teaching is an expansion of the Beatitude, '*Blessed are the pure in heart...*' (2). He explained impurity of heart as that which seeks outward

(1) Matthew 6; (2) Matthew 5:8.

recognition for good deeds, pretentiousness in prayer, and fasting to gain kudos with men. Such things disqualify a believer from the unity of heaven's reward (1). He went on to accentuate the need for focus and singleness of heart (2) and the avoidance of dual loyalties (3). He closed this theme in His teaching by addressing the need to avoid divided thinking through undue '*worry*', or as the King James Bible has it, '*taking thought*' (4). Rather interesting in this mix is His repeated emphasis on forgiveness (5). Could it be that we have not recognized that the reason that unforgiveness gives ground to the enemy (6) is because it creates a division of heart? It's a judgment in a bed of grace.

The Kingdom and Righteousness

At the climax of this teaching on unity Jesus makes a statement that would be easily misunderstood were it not for the context in which it is found. He says,

'*But seek ye first the kingdom of God, and His righteousness; and all these things shall be added unto you.*'

Matthew 6:33

We could think Jesus is asking believers to embrace two separate things here: [1] the kingdom of God and [2] His righteousness. However, context prohibits that interpretation. Jesus is not going to teach on the power of unity and then interject a random dualist concept. What this means is that '*the kingdom of God*' and '*His righteousness*' must share a common thread. Hold that thought.

(1) Matthew 6:1-4, 5-6, 16; (2) Matthew 6:19-21; 22-23; (3) Matthew 6:24; (4) Matthew 6:25-34; (5) Matthew 6:12, 14-15; (6) Matthew 18:23-35.

The words here which derail many, are 'His righteousness'. Because righteousness is obedience to a command/ment (1) many assume that its use in the Sermon on the Mount (TSOTM) is reference to the Law. Therefore, this verse is usually expounded along these lines: that because we are no longer under the law, and because Christ is our righteousness (and we are found in Him) it is logical that we are therefore, in 'His righteousness'. Having apparently met that requirement the verse is then effectively minimized to say, 'Seek first the kingdom of God'. Unfortunately, that is not what is intended here. That line of thinking does not accommodate the Apostle John's latter teaching where he says,

> 'Little children, let no one deceive you.
> He who practices righteousness is righteous,
> just as He is righteous.'
>
> 1 John 3:7

What better fits the context, and is consistent with the rest of Jesus' teaching on the mount, is something altogether different.

Another influence that conditions us to misinterpret this verse is an earlier verse in TSOTM that also talks of the need for righteousness. This is where Jesus said,

> '...that except your righteousness shall exceed the righteousness of
> the scribes and Pharisees,
> ye shall in no case enter into the kingdom of heaven.'
>
> Matthew 5:20

1) Romans 6:16; TSOTM = The Sermon on The Mount

89

Understandably, this too is taken as a reference to the keeping of Old Testament Law. Why else would Jesus make reference to the scribes and Pharisees? This sort of reasoning on the subject of righteousness has many thinking that the whole of TSOTM is Old Testament and therefore practically irrelevant to us as New Covenant believers.

I suggest that there is another way to view these and other references to righteousness in the New Testament. There are two kinds, or levels of righteousness. There is legal righteousness that Jesus met fully, and there is revelatory righteousness. Revelatory righteousness is the foundational level of righteousness that is first found in Abraham, who, *'believed God and it was accounted to him for righteousness'* (1). *'His righteousness'* is righteousness at heart level, not that which is achieved through outward observance of the law (Jesus has already met that requirement). Earlier we discovered that the context of Jesus' directive to *'seek first the kingdom of God and His righteousness'* means that there is a link between these two elements. The link is that revelatory righteousness leads to a manifestation of the kingdom and all its provision, this is what is meant by *'entering the kingdom'*. Putting that another way, if our heart seeks after His heart (the kingdom within), then revelation is released to our spirit, which if acted upon (righteousness) will manifest the kingdom (all these things added to you).

If we consider that Jesus called the Pharisees hypocrites (2) – people who profess right living but whose heart attitudes contradict that - then His requirement that we exceed their level of righteousness is not about outward observation of the law, but

(1) Romans 4:3; Galatians 3:6; James 2:23; (2) Matthew 23:13-29.

rather an inward application of the revelation He supplies. For it is only through heart obedience that entry is gained into the kingdom.

There are two levels of righteousness:
Legal righteousness and
Revelatory righteousness

Righteousness, Peace and Joy

An appreciation of the two layers of righteousness brings a new depth of understanding to Paul's writings,

'For the kingdom of God is not meat and drink;
but righteousness, and peace, and joy in the Holy Ghost.'
Romans 14:17

Notice here that Paul is contrasting the regulation of outward observance - meat and drink - with life in the Spirit (outward vs inward). There is an evident progression in *'righteousness, peace and joy'* that comes alive when we recognize the existence of revelatory righteousness.

Righteousness > Peace > Joy

It begins with a revelation released to the heart of man, that when acted upon brings us into righteousness (obedience to the rhema word). The flow on from this is peace in the heart. The Hebrew word for *peace* is 'Shalom'. In Hebrew this is spelled with four letters, (שָׁלוֹם) Sheen, Lamed, Vav and Mem.

שַׁ: Sheen (pictured as teeth): Devour, consume, **destroy**.
ל: Lamed (pictured as a staff): Leadership, **authority**
ו: Vav: (pictured as a nail): And, anchored, **established**
ם: Mem: (pictured as a body of water): Massive, **chaos**

Therefore at its root Shalom can be understood to mean, 'Destroy the authority that establishes chaos'. When we receive and correctly apply the revelation supplied it destroys the authority that establishes chaos in a situation. Selah. Adding to this insight on peace are Jesus' words,

> *'Think not that I am come to send peace on earth:*
> *I came not to send peace, but a sword.'*
>
> Matthew 10:34

Here Jesus contrasts peace with a sword. Elsewhere in Luke's Gospel the same verse is recorded as,

> *'Suppose ye that I am come to give peace on earth?*
> *I tell you, Nay; but rather division.'*
>
> Luke 12:51

Here peace is contrasted with division. Jesus is saying that His words polarize people. His declaration confirms what we saw earlier: that a 'word' has the power to bring division. However, we also comprehend from this that '*peace*', as the opposite of '*division*', must result from unity. True peace is a union between us and God. So, combining the original meaning of shalom and our understanding of peace as unity with God we see that revelatory righteousness has the power to destroy wrongful and divisive authorities that cause chaos in a person's heart or situation. The end result according to the Apostle Paul is that revelatory righteousness promotes our union with God which in turn produces joy. Now that is the joy of the Lord that is our strength!

The Superiority of Revelatory Righteousness

Revelatory righteousness is not new. It existed all the way through the Old Testament even in the midst of the controlling regulation of the Law. Abraham sacrificed his son; Jericho was destroyed despite the army traveling further than was permitted on the Sabbath; Samson ate honey from a dead carcass and married a Gentile bride; Ruth was a Moabitess; David faced Goliath when he was too young to go to war; he also ate the showbread; Elijah was fed by unclean birds; Elisha lay on a dead body; Isaiah walked around naked for three years; Ezekiel ate food prepared on fires of dung; Hosea married a harlot and Jesus healed on the Sabbath, etc. All of which could be construed as against the Law.

It was revelatory righteousness that carried Elisha on to receive the prized mantle even though his master had repeatedly

(1) James 2:13.

told him to wait at each intervening step in their fateful last journey together (1). Staying behind would have been proven Elisha's righteous obedience to his master's command, but the revelation of his master's rapture carried him onward.

It should be evident that revelatory righteousness was and is often God's vehicle for breakthrough. God's heart standard of righteousness, otherwise called, '*His righteousness*' has always held a higher place in God than outward regulatory observance. Just as mercy triumphs over judgment(2) so revelatory righteousness is superior to regulatory righteousness because it emanates from the heart of God.

Mercy	Revelatory Righteousness
Judgment	Regulatory Righteousness

A Hunger and Thirst for Righteousness

If, at this point, you are thinking that this gives the green light to every independent-spirited individual to justify their stance of non-accountability, be assured it does not. The call for us to '*hunger and thirst after righteousness*' (3), provides the correction and balance in what may otherwise result in new levels of unbridled license. For '*hunger*' is reference to the written word, while '*thirst*' is related to the revelatory word of the Spirit of God. We hunger for the bread of God's word and we thirst for the living water of the Spirit (4). The written word is still our standard for daily faith and practice while we seek the revelation of the Spirit for individual matters.

(1) 2 KIngs 2:1-14; (2) James 2:13; (3) Matthew 5:6; (4) Amos 8:11; John 7:37-39.

SUMMARY

1) If you can divide you can conquer.
2) Division is the most overt and covert of spiritual strategies.
3) We divide offensively when we decree and declare the rhema word.
4) We are divided when:
    (1) Words divide our head and heart
    (2) We criticize our colleagues
    (3) Busy-ness distracts us from revelatory truth.
5) Unity empowers us to see fruit.
6) Where the king is, there is the kingdom
7) One of the main focuses of TSOTM was the importance of unity.
8) Unforgiveness divides the heart and gives the enemy ground.
9) There are two kinds of righteousness:
    (1) Legal
    (2) Revelatory
10) Revelatory righteousness is the key to the fruit of the kingdom of God
11) Righteousness > Peace > Joy is a progression.
12) Shalom means destroy the authority that establishes chaos.
13) Peace as the opposite of division speaks of union with God.
14) Revelatory righteousness > Oneness with God > Joy in our heart.
15) Revelatory righteousness is often the vehicle for breakthrough.
16) Revelatory righteousness supersedes regulatory righteousness.
17) We '*hunger*' for the bread of God's written word.
18) We '*thirst*' for the living water of the Spirit.
19) The two - hunger and thirst - bring balance.
20) The word of God is still our standard for faith and practice as we seek revelation for individual matters.

CHAPTER EIGHT

An Invitation to Sonship

Isaac Centerstage

Isaac lived 180 years, the longest of all the patriarchs, yet there is less written about him than the others. There are twelve chapters written about Abraham, Jacob and Joseph, but there is only one that has Isaac center stage. Our spotlight is brought to focus on Genesis 26, where we encounter Isaac re-digging the wells his father had dug. This passage of Scripture is vital because it portrays the journey to sonship. Like us, at the outset he is but an heir (1), yet his successful campaign to dig wells against persistent opposition saw him sow seed as a son and ultimately receive a hundredfold return during drought. This passage of Scripture with its emphasis on the 'digging' of wells is a flashing neon sign inviting us to go deeper. Please read Genesis Chapter 26.

1) Genesis 24:36.

I set to study this chapter when a couple of prophetic friends came to me separately and asked what the passage taught about the keys to unlocking prosperity in potentially trying financial times. What I came away with was not so much a set of principles to bolster one's financial position, though they are to be found here, but rather that real prosperity is anchored to a deeper walk with and commitment to God.

Sojourners and Dwellers

Given that our focus is on unveiling and entering the kingdom, and that Gerar is the borderland between Canaan (The Promised Land) and Egypt, what unfolds here for Isaac has relevance for us today. Earlier, God instructed Isaac not to go down to Egypt. God had to tell Isaac this because that's where Isaac was headed in his heart. Like his father before him, his default setting was to turn to the world, rather than to God, when under trial. After this directive from God, he was also told to 'sojourn' in the land (1). However, we read later that he chose instead to 'dwell' in the land (2). The difference is not immediately obvious. The Hebrew for '*Sojourn*' is 'Gur' (Gimel, Vav, Reysh), that is 'Foreigner', or literally 'Camel man'. Whereas the Hebrew translated '*Dwell*' is 'Yasab', meaning 'To sit, to stay, to endure'. It appears that Isaac chose to settle and made it his home, instead of maintaining an, 'I'm just passing through' heart-attitude. Though an heir he still clung to the world around him not having fully grasped that heaven was his home.

(1) Genesis 26:3; (2) Genesis 26:6.

Spotting the Overview

In reading through the passage it is important to realize that verses 12-15 are in parenthesis, that is, they are a summary of what is about to unfold. It is easy to miss this in our Western linear style of thinking. As a good teacher, one of God's methods is to first provide an overview before filling out the details in the material that follows. For example, we saw Him summarise His creation in the first verse of Genesis and then lay out the essential elements in the rest of chapter one. And again we saw Him release the Beatitudes as a preview to the details in the Sermon on the Mount. In the same way God gives an overview of Isaac's prosperity to make us hungry to dig deeper. The key to spotting this 'break in proceedings' is:

- Acknowledging that it requires water for seed to grow and Isaac hadn't dug his first well until verse 19;
- Recognizing time and a process is involved - he '*started to prosper*', he '*continued to prosper*' until he '*became extremely prosperous*' (1); and finally,
- Spotting that the information supplied in verse 15 about the wells is repeated in verse 18, only this time with a different emphasis.

The Promise

Isaac, as heir, is promised a blessing because of the obedience of his father (2), we are in a similar position having arrived as

(1) Genesis 26:13; (2) Genesis 26:3-5.

heirs by faith in Jesus Christ (1). This means that, like Isaac, we are invited into the accelerated growth to become mature sons by following the outline in this passage (2). It is encouraging to find that though Isaac had been there '*a long time*' as an heir (3), in moving through the wells he matured to the place where he sowed and saw a hundredfold return in one year (4).

The Surface Lessons

Reading through the chapter there are initial observations to be gleaned, noted and learned from before going deeper. Firstly, God used physical need (famine) and opposition to grow Isaac spiritually. Next, it appears he fell into the same weakness as his father by calling his wife, Rebekah, his sister. Then, even though he had favor and promise before God, this alone did not stop opposing forces from trying to steal his inheritance from him. Finally, he named the wells by the same names his father had given them. This implies that each generation needs to discover and dig these same wells regardless of their spiritual pedigree. Indeed, many a movement has been birthed by an apostle only to have successive generations lose momentum and focus because they have never had to dig the same wells.

Unveiling a Kingdom Key

This passage is intriguing in that despite Isaac being promised multiplication of physical seed (flesh and blood offspring) (5), he is actually blessed with compounding plant seed (kernels) (6).

(1) 1 Corinthians 1:30; Philippians 3:9; Hebrews 11:8; (2) John 1:12; (3) Genesis 26:8; (4) Genesis 26:12; (5) Genesis 26:4; (6) Genesis 26:12.

This should get our attention because what looks to be the promise manifesting in a different area, is potentially the key to an inter-dimensional kingdom truth. Hidden in the physical miracle is a deeper spiritual principle. To unearth the spiritual root of this apparent anomaly requires that other Scriptures be overlaid to see what Holy Spirit is saying (1). So the task is to consider relevant scriptures relating to wells, seed and water to see - by overlaying them in our narrative - whether they may bring a deeper hue to what is painted on the surface.

***Every generation needs to dig
Isaac's wells regardless of their
spiritual pedigree***

From the Book of Proverbs we discover that, '*The words of a man's mouth are as deep waters*' (2), and Jesus said that '*The seed is the word of God*' (3). He also promised that the water He gave would become '*a well of water springing up*' (4), and that rivers of living water would flow out of the belly of believers (5). This means that the spirit of man is a well, drawing living water from another realm, out of sight and independent of the area into which it flows. So that Isaac's promise of many offspring being reflected in the multiplication of plant seed (which represent words from his mouth), tells us we reproduce in accordance with the words of our mouth (6). Not just any words, but words drawn from the heart. Following on from this discovery, could it be that Isaac's wells are stages of discovery within himself and that the water flowing from

1) 1 Corinthians 2:13b; (2) Proverbs 18:4; (3) Luke 8:11; (4) John 4:14; (5) John 7:37-39; (6) f. Genesis 1:11 & Psalm 1:3;

the wells is as the Spirit of God giving Him revelation? It is here that the context of the story will aid in confirming, or otherwise, our search for insights beyond the surface.

Isaac and Abimelech

There is an interesting 'on-off-on again' relationship between Abimelech and Isaac. It started with Isaac living amongst or finding shelter with Abimelech and the Philistines of Gerar, before the king confronted him on the fact that Rebekah was not his sister, but his wife. At which point the two part company only to have Abimelech seek him out with two nobles from his court to cut covenant with him because they acknowledge the hand of God on him. The timing of this union indicates some deeper meaning because it takes place after Isaac has built an altar, pitched his tent and begun to dig the final well (Beersheba). God's hand seemed to be on this coming together because the well only brought forth its life-giving water after the agreement had been struck between the two parties.

The Journey through the Wells

The key to this episode in the life of Isaac is his onward journey through the wells. The meaning of the names of the wells reveals a progression that runs in sync with Isaac's growing prosperity.

Esek

The first well, Esek, which is named after the events surrounding its discovery, means 'Contention'. As such, it depicts a claim and counter-claim tug of war over the appearance of the life-giving water of revelation. Earlier in the narrative we read that the Philistines had stopped and filled the wells with earth (1). This is a picture of spiritual forces attempting to stop the flow of the Spirit of revelation by blocking it with the physical and natural thoughts of the flesh. The contention that took place is a picture of seesawing doubt, where the world battles against the word of faith. Peter visited this place when he stepped out on Jesus' word to, '*Come*' and then the wind and the waves overpowered Jesus' word so that he began to sink (2). James addresses this same issue when he writes, '*A double-minded man is unstable in all his ways*' (3). Esek, then, depicts the early stage of spiritual growth where a believer receives a word of revelation but circumstance and natural physical constraints attempt to usurp the authority of the rhema word received.

Sitnah

Isaac's next well is similarly met with resistance. This time he calls the place, 'Sitnah', a name that has its roots in the thought of 'Legal accusation'. Once an heir gets a taste of what they are entitled to the enemy comes to challenge its legality through religious regulation and control. Jesus confronted this type of resistance when the Pharisees, Sadducees and Scribes threw Scripture at

(1) Genesis 26:15; (2) Matthew 14:29; (3) James 1:8.

Him in an attempt to discredit His teaching and challenge His authority(1).

Sitnah accounts for the multitude of prophetic people who come to Christ by revelation of grace only to have religious spirits deceive them into religious form and duty. As a consequence many of these would-be seers and prophets look elsewhere for spiritual fulfilment and find themselves journeying through the New Age in search of meaningful expression.

> *Many people come to Christ*
> *but move away into the*
> *New Age to find expression*
> *after religious people try*
> *to fit them into their mold*

In more traditional settings many Christians fall prey to the same religious limitation when they over intellectualise the supernatural. Their attempts to reason and explain it away result in abdication from entering the kingdom through a life of faith.

Rehoboth

Like his previous stopovers not much is recorded openly about Isaac's next location. However, there is plenty that can be extrapolated to bring understanding of the role Rehoboth played on his journey. This was the first place where there was no opposition, where Isaac first discovered room to move and recognised his potential fruitfulness.

(1) Matthew 19:3-8; 21:15-16; 22:23-32.

'And he removed from there, and dug another well; and for that they strove not: and he called the name of it Rehoboth; and he said, For now the Lord hath made room for us, and we shall be fruitful in the land.'

Genesis 26:22

The significance Rehoboth carries is the thought of 'Roomy' or 'Spaciousness'. The Hebrew for 'roomy' is three letters (רְחַב), רְ: Reysh = Man, חַ: Chet = Wall, ב:Bet = House. The last two letters combined (Chet, Bet) spell, 'Inner chamber', so that the journey to Rehoboth announces discovery of the 'Man of the Inner Chamber'. This is the place where the believer discovers the 'room' of heaven's provision within, or as Jesus put it, *'the kingdom of God is within you'* (1).

As good Pentecostal believers it is tempting here to paint over this temporary campsite as solely the discovery of speaking in tongues. While that facet of spiritual growth is represented here it would be an injustice to a son's path to maturity if this scene was clothed with a manifestation of the Spirit of God without having a deeper appreciation of its foundation.

It is interesting to note that in writing this passage Holy Spirit records that it was Isaac's servants who dug the first two wells but that *'he'* (Isaac) dug the one at Rehoboth (2), even though it is likely that the servants physically dug it. With the preceding insight on the Hebrew origins of 'Roominess' as 'The man of the inner chamber' it is worth acknowledging that the first well (Esek) appears to deal with opposition of a natural and physical nature.

The well at Sitnah addresses religious opposition aimed at

(1) Luke 17:21; (2) Genesis 26:22.

the areas of the mind and thought life. Included in this bag of soul-level battles are our Scriptural conversations with cultists at the front door and those limited to an intellectual pursuit of God (1).

Rehoboth marks the search for life-giving water on a deeper and more personal level, namely, in Isaac's (and the believer's) spirit. Together, these three wells move through the areas of body, soul and spirit in an ever deepening thirst for revelation life from God.

Running parallel with that is an increasing yielding of one's being unto God. Rehoboth marks the discovery of the voice of the Spirit at another level beyond preconceived efforts to direct and frame up His 'word' ourselves. It's the place where the mysteries of God are communicated symbolically. It's where meditative thought results in life-giving revelation that produces fruit. Its when you recognize God is speaking to you when you may wake up with a song in your head, when a person's name comes to mind out of the blue, when you continually see the same series of numbers, when you awaken after a dream, when you will hear two people use an obscure phrase within a short space of time, when you will see something strangely unseasonal, when you will see something that you have never seen before as you go about your everyday activity. And the list goes on...

Whilst I have chosen not to focus on speaking in tongues here, it would be remiss of me not to mention it, because the lack of opposition at Rehoboth practically broadcasts its use anyway. Rehoboth marks the revelation that we are able to pray in the Spirit at times when we either don't know what or how to pray for a given situation, and when we tend to over think or second-guess

(1) cf. 1 Corinthains 4:20.

106

urselves before God. There is no opposition because praying in
he Spirit overcomes our mental limitations and the only recourse
or spiritual opposition is to bow the knee.

The Apostle Paul describes such outpourings from this
waterhole when he says,

*Howbeit we speak wisdom among them that are perfect (full and wanting in nothing):
'et not the wisdom of this world, nor of the princes of this world, that come to naught:
But we speak the wisdom of God in a mystery, even the hidden wisdom, which God
ordained before the world unto our glory...*

*But as it is written, Eye hath not seen, nor ear heard, neither have entered into the heart
of man, the things which God hath prepared for them that love him.*

*But God hath revealed them unto us by his Spirit: for the Spirit searches all things, yes,
the deep things of God. For what man knows the things of a man, save the spirit of man
which is in him?*

Even so the things of God knows no man, but the Spirit of God.

*Now we have received, not the spirit of the world, but the Spirit which is of God; that we
might know the things that are freely given to us of God.*

*Which things also we speak, not in the words which man's wisdom teaches, but which
the Holy Ghost teaches; comparing (and combining) spiritual things with spiritual.*

*But the natural man receives not the things of the Spirit of God: for they are foolishness
unto him: neither can he know them, because they are spiritually discerned.'*

1 Corinthians 2:6-14 (emphasis added)

In an intellectual pursuit of God many people attempt to
bypass this waterhole not realizing that:

All are called to be prophetic (1);
All are exhorted to child-like faith(2);
All are destined to bring heaven to earth (3).

His discovery at Reheboth took Isaac to another level because
he text records that his next move was '*up*' to Beersheba(4). It will

1) Numbers 11:23; (2) Matthew 18:3-4; (3) Matthew 6:10; (4) Genesis 26:23.

be evident from what follows that Beersheba represents a quantum shift in the maturity of a son. In recording that Isaac's servants dug the first two wells, I suggest that the body and soul are meant to be servants to the real 'you' - your spirit man. The progression through the first two wells amplifies that a believer will have to overcome opposition both from without - in the natural realm - and from within - mentally - to discover and plumb the reservoir that is available through our spirit.

Peter

If we were to trace this journey through the life of Peter, Esek would equate with his faltering at the physical threat presented by the wind and waves after stepping out on Jesus' revelatory word to '*Come*'. The religious opposition that is encountered at Sitnah parallels the time when Jesus' followers were abandoning Him en masse. At that time Jesus stated that believers would be marked by those who ate His flesh, and drank His blood, which was an extremely confrontational thought by most standards, but especially to Jews under the Law. However, in the face of those offended by this teaching and leaving, Peter stayed the course. When Jesus asked whether he and the others disciples also wanted to leave he had obviously considered his options before he replied, '*Where else can we go? You have the words of eternal life*'. Hence he was not swayed by the religious voices disputing Jesus' words because they took Him literally, but rather held to the Lord because he recognized the supremacy of revelation over religion. The equivalent of Rehoboth for Peter was when he declared that Jesus was, '*the Christ, the Son of the Living God!*' Jesus response to that was that he did not arrive at that answer through any reasoning or coaching by men, but by revelation to his spirit directly from the Father. At this stage, we might assume Peter's progress and position was assured especially after the following affirmation and commendation from Christ,

'*And I say also unto you, That you are Peter,*
and upon this rock I will build my church;
and the gates of hell shall not prevail against it.
And I will give unto you the keys of the kingdom of heaven...'
Matthew 16:18-19

However, before the ink had time to dry on his apparent promotion amongst the disciples Jesus had to rebuke him for trying to dissuade Him from His sacrificial rendezvous with Jerusalem. In this instance, Jesus declared Peter was being used of satan and mindful only of the things of men (1). If this parallel between Peter and Isaac is correct it tells us that without a further move to Beersheba we may be prone to think we have arrived before it is an actual reality. It also suggests that it is one thing to receive revelation from God, but quite another to know whether an ensuing course of action is spirit-led or merely looks good and sits nicely with our personal agenda. Whatever is on offer it would pay to take our time and check 'in' with God before continuing. Israel's covenant with the Gibeonites attests to the same truth on a corporate level (2). The next chapter is dedicated to the final step to full sonship as portrayed in the journey to Beersheba.

(1) Matthew 16:21-23; (2) Joshua 9:1-27.

109

SUMMARY:

(1) Isaac's journey through the wells is an invitation to sonship.

(2) We are called to be sojourners not dwellers.

(3) Give an overview before filling out the details to your students.

(4) Isaac parallels us in that he was a son of promise because of the obedience of his father.

(5) Genesis 26 surface lessons:

> (1) Physical need stretched and grew Isaac spiritually.
>
> (2) God's favor did not stop spiritual opposition.
>
> (3) Each generation needs to dig the wells of our forefathers.

(6) We reproduce according to the words of our mouth.

(7) The wells are stages of inner discovery for Isaac.

(8) Esek means 'Contention' and is where the flow of revelation is first challenged and blocked by physical and natural thoughts of the flesh.

(9) Sitnah: means 'Legal accusation' and is where religious spirits try to regulate, control and usurp the revelatory word.

(10) Rehoboth is the discovery of the 'Man of the inner chamber'.

(11) Each well relates to man's tri-partite nature. Esek: the body; Sitnah: the soul; Rehoboth: the spirit.

(12) Rehoboth marks the discovery of the voice of the Spirit.

(13) All are called to be prophetic, all are exhorted to child-like faith, all are destined to bring heaven to earth.

(14) Your body and soul are to be servants to the real you: your spirit.

(15) Every believer will need to overcome opposition from within and without.

(16) We are prone to think we have arrived before it is an actual reality.

(17) Always check with God before committing to a major new course of action.

CHAPTER NINE

For Many are Called...

Our understanding of the journey to sonship is more fully rounded when we trace the life of other notable Bible characters as they traverse the path mapped out by Isaac. Just as believers who have come to Calvary's cross are partakers of a promise to rule and reign with Him, so Joseph and David also received prophetic promises that they would reign. Jacob's gift of a coat of many colors was a prophetic act of the glory in which he would someday be shrouded and David's anointing by the prophet Samuel declared his future kingship. Both men walked through repeated levels of opposition before they arrived at their prophetic destinies.

For the sake of brevity we will only consider Joseph here. After a revelatory dream (which confirmed his father's prophetic gesture) Joseph visited Esek, in type, when he was physically separated from the scene of the promise and sold off to Egypt by his brothers. His journey to Sitnah took place when, as the prosperous overseer of Potiphar's household with the evident blessing of the Lord over all he was in charge of, he was suddenly accused of sexual misconduct. To understand how this incident relates to Sitnah we need to appreciate the scene on another level. In metaphoric terms humans may at times be pictured as a house (1). An extension of that understanding is that the woman of the household may also prefigure the spirit of the person (explained later in this chapter). When Joseph was given charge as overseer of all of Potiphar's household it was a picture of the soul of the natural man governing a person's life. He was at the religious, soul-governed level of development. This was his Sitnah, and in this place any accusation of sexual impropriety is the equivalent of a cry of spiritual misconduct.

In prison Joseph was positioned for his Rehoboth moment. Here he was in the place of revelation when he accurately interpreted the dreams of 'a bread-maker' who was broken and hung on a tree, and 'a wine-bearer', who was in a pit before being resurrected. I believe it was during those two long years when his circumstances did not change, that he became transparent before God and truly plumbed the depths of Rehoboth. The book of Genesis confirms this when it writes,

'Joseph is a fruitful bough, even a fruitful bough by a well;
whose branches run over the wall.'

Genesis 49:22

Joseph's fruitfulness, like Isaac's and Peter's, fully manifested when

(1) 2 Corinthians 5:1.

ne moved on from Rehoboth and went '*up*' to Beersheba.

Beersheba

For Isaac, Beersheba represents a new level of yielding before God. It was here that the Bible records he built his first altar and pitched his tent. The altar speaks of the sacrifice of his heart, and the tent refers to his life given in abandonment to God (1). That he went '*up*' to Beersheba strongly suggests that this move is representative of entering the eternal realm. This is further confirmed in the life of Abraham, who had earlier walked the same path, and at Beersheba called on the Lord as *The Eternal God* (2). Previously there had been no mention of an altar for Isaac in Gerar. Its construction at Beersheba declared a deeper relationship with God. In alignment with this is the establishment of a covenant with Abimelech. It will become evident that this relationship symbolized more than the earthly fulfilment of a universal promise of God,

> '*When a man's ways please the Lord,*
> *He makes even his enemies to be at peace with him.'*
>
> Proverbs 16:7

Abimelech: Father of the King

To fully appreciate the meaning of moving up to Beersheba we must first backtrack to consider Isaac's interaction with Abimelech. There is more going on here than first meets the eye. God is using the surface interplay between Isaac and Abimelech

---

1) Romans 12:1; (2) Genesis 21:33.

in this passage to illustrate the underlying spiritual connection between Himself and Isaac. The story outlines a relationship that started out as one of convenience for Isaac, but finished in a union with Abimelech, Phichol and Ahuzzath. Considering the meaning of the name, 'Abimelech', which means 'Father of the king', he is immediately symbolised as God the Father, but this raises the issues of Isaac being sent away and whether a non-Israelite could ever represent God. Is there a precedent of a non-Israelite representing God? Well, what about Pharaoh? Not Moses' Pharaoh, but Joseph's Pharaoh. Didn't Joseph sit at Pharaoh's right-hand distributing seed as a picture of Jesus at the right hand of the Father? So there is a precedent.

How then does one explain Isaac's deception regarding his wife, Rebekah, and the rift between Abimelech and Isaac? After comparing Isaac's lies with Abraham's about Sarah it is evident that both father and son sinned in the same area. The plot thickens when we consider that Abraham also lied to Abimelech (1). Remember, underneath the surface story there is an even more compelling spiritual one. Is this a generational problem? To answer that question and to understand what was portrayed in these incidents an appreciation of personification is needed. Personification is used extensively in Hebrew poetry, where a person can represent a city, country, church, virtue or the like, just as wisdom is seen as a lady calling out in the streets (2). Piecing together the Psalmist's repeatedly used expression, '*My glory rejoices*' (3) in reference to his spirit being overcome in delight, with Paul's teaching that a wife is '*the glory of her husband*' (4), points to the idea that Rebekah is symbolic of Isaac's spirit. This is supported by the fact

(1) Genesis 20:2ff; (2) Proverbs 1:20; (3) Psalm 16:9; 30:12; 57:8; 108:1; (4) 1 Corinthians 11:7.

that a husband and wife are one flesh (1). Isaac, in fear, lying about his wife was relating that he and his spirit were not united. The Scripture addresses that rift between us and God when it says,

'For to be carnally minded is death;
but to be spiritually minded is life and peace.
Because the carnal mind is enmity against God...'

Romans 8:6-8

Isaac was *'a long time'* (2) in a place where his heart and head were not in alignment, so God confronted him with a revelation: Abimelech looking through a window and pointing out the lie. This repeated lying by the son was not so much a generational curse coming down through Abraham, but rather the propensity of man to deny the voice of his own spirit in the face of threat or pressure (3). Jesus said, *'If you deny Me before men, I also will deny you before My Father in heaven'.* We normally associate this verse with witnessing, but it has a broader application if we consider Jesus as 'the Word'. Namely, words not rooted in Christ here on earth, have no backing from heaven. The positive side of this is that words from the Spirit of God do have the whole of heaven behind them.

God confronted Isaac on the disharmony between his head and heart because words need to be drawn from our heart to be effective. This alignment prepared Isaac for his journey of discovery through the wells. The Hebrew word for 'Truth' is Emet', (אֱמֶת) and is made up of three letters, א: Aleph, מ: Mem and ת: Tav. Jewish teachers explain the meaning of the word through

(1) Ephesians 5:31; (2) Genesis 26:8; (3) cf. 1 Corinthians 6:17.

each letter's position in the alphabet. These are at the beginning, middle and the end of the Hebrew alphabet. Therefore, truth is like having the three tumblers of a lock in alignment so that access is granted. In other words, truth is having the same on the inside as what's outside, or when your heart and head say the same thing. A lie is when you say one thing and your heart another. Only when your heart and head say the same thing can you effectively sow words and see a return (1). This was the secret to Samuel having no words fall to the ground (2). He heard from God before he opened his mouth to speak and the Spirit of truth empowered his words so they did not return void (3).

Truth is when your
head and heart are in alignment
and say the same thing

Why then did Abimelech say, '*Go from us, because you are mightier than we*' (4)? The word, '*Mighty*' (Hebrew: Asam), here has a double meaning. It does mean, 'Many', but it also means 'To close' or 'Cover' the eyes. In the natural, Abimelech said this because when Abraham lied to him about his wife, Sarah, all their orifices were closed. Modern Bibles say simply that the Philistines stopped child bearing (5). However, Hebrew commentaries suggest that all their orifices were closed, which would certainly solicit a faster response. The prospect of revisiting that was too much for Abimelech. Spiritually, God had to reveal to Isaac that his own eye (his spirit) was effectively covered and required a cataract removed

(1) cf. John 14:17; 15:26; 16:13; (2) 1 Samuel 3:19; (3) Isaiah 55:11; (4) Genesis 26:16; (5) Genesis 20:16-17.

so that He could fulfil the promise of multiplication in his life (1). Once there was alignment within he could be released to unearth the well of his spirit by walking through the stages in the journey to Beersheba. Leaving Gerar, Abimelech's country, meant that where he had once been comfortable in being supplied water, he was now forced to dig for his own. He had to be discomforted because only those who thirst are filled (2). Though the bursting forth of life-giving revelation is a son's livelihood and provision, he is usually prepared for breakthrough by being disquieted.

Joseph and Peter

When Joseph was working for Potiphar, at the equivalent of his Sitnah, his reasoning against an act of sexual misconduct was revealing. The Bible records that he had no interest in his master's wife's advances for two reasons: firstly, he honored the trust given him and placed the integrity of Potiphar's household above personal gratification, and secondly, he wanted to maintain spiritual integrity with God (3). Both motives are godly, but in considering Potiphar's reputation ahead of God's Joseph had things in the wrong order. Jesus said, '*He who loves father or mother more than me is not worthy of Me*' (4). Even though Joseph had done the right thing, the greatness of the call upon his life, demanded more than correct outward performance. God wanted his heart. As he proceeded in his journey of interpreting the butler and baker's dreams, he put God first when he said, '*Do not interpretations belong to God, tell them to me*'. However, having correctly interpreted the dreams the core of his being is again on display when he follows up

(1) Genesis 26:3-4. (2) Matthew 5:6; (3) Genesis 39:9; (4) Matthew 10:37.

the interpretation by saying,

> *'But think on <u>me</u> when it shall be well with you,*
> *and show kindness, I pray, unto <u>me</u>,*
> *and make mention of <u>me</u> unto Pharaoh,*
> *and bring <u>me</u> out of this house:*
> *For indeed <u>I</u> was stolen away out of the land of the Hebrews:*
> *and here also have <u>I</u> done nothing*
> *that they should put <u>me</u> into the dungeon.'*
>
> Genesis 40:14-15

His priorities revealed that even though he could *'understand all mysteries'* and was living in a godly manner he was still occupying the throne of his life. This is Joseph before he broke through to his Beersheba.

When he was brought before Pharaoh to interpret his dream the Scriptures record that he first shaved and changed his clothing (1). While there are natural reasons why he would clean himself up before a royal appearance, there was also a spiritual message hidden here. Shaving is a picture of him removing any semblance of the flesh, and changing his garb is indicative of the new man he has become. Finally, in standing before Pharaoh, he says, *'It is not in me, God will give Pharaoh an answer of peace'*. Previously, God had been *'with'* him (and there was associated blessing with this (2). However, during this audience with the king of Egypt, Pharaoh himself caught the magnitude of the shift that had taken place in Joseph. Pharaoh said, *'Can we find such a one as this, a man <u>in whom is</u> the Spirit of God'* (3). Could it be that God's image

(1) Genesis 41:14; (2) Genesis 39:2, 21, 23; (3) Genesis 41:38.

of a mature son is one who reflects the Father in such likeness and intensity as to make His very essence present? I believe Jesus succinctly summarized the journey to Beersheba, or full sonship, when He said,

> '*He who finds his life will lose it,*
> *and he who loses his life for My sake will find it*'.
> Matthew 10:39

This verse really captures the essence of the final step - Rehoboth to Beersheba. Hence, Joseph gave his life to God in prison. It finally dawned on him that the message to the butler and baker through their dreams also applied to him; in short, he had to 'die' to be resurrected. He realized he was no longer a prisoner to his past, and with that revelation came much more than just his physical freedom.

For Isaac, the last hurdle to Beersheba came a little differently. On being pushed further and further away from the mindset of 'dwelling', he embraced 'sojourning', where he discovered that there were no constraints on 'the man of the inner chamber'. With that revelation came the realization of the access that was now available within, causing him to proclaim, '*Now... we shall be fruitful in the land*'. Isaac is a picture of the man who found treasure in a field and went and sold all he had to purchase it (1). We have already seen how his servants dug the first two wells but that he excavated at Rehoboth to convey the new commitment of his spirit man. At Beersheba, the text takes another turn and records that his servants

1) Matthew 13:44.

were again those employed in digging for water. However, this was not an indication of less personal involvement by Isaac, but one of greater commitment as he now laid his whole being down as a servant of God, offering up his complete body, soul and spirit on the altar. Beersheba means 'well of the oath' or 'well of the seven' the two are connected because both are based on a word that depicts a circle. Just as the days of the week complete their cycle after seven days so an oath is the completion of a cycle. An oath begins with words and ends when it is fulfilled. If we considered Jesus'

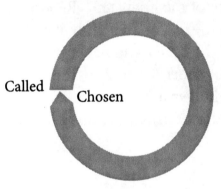

words, '*For many are called, but few chosen*' (1), Beersheba is arriving at being '*chosen*'. It is that point when there's completion of a cycle, where our life joins the destiny for which it was called. Like seed sown he stepped across that final threshold when he abandoned himself unto God. As Christ explained,

Except a corn of wheat fall into the ground and die,
it abides alone:
but if it die, it brings forth much fruit.
He that loves his life shall lose it;
and he that hates his life in this world
shall keep it unto life eternal.

John 12:24-25

Even though Peter had tasted Rehoboth's provision when

(1) Matthew 22:14; (2) Matthew 17:27.

Jesus received the tax money from the fish's mouth (2), his move to Beersheba came later. For him the final step was precipitated by his humbling by Christ's foreknowledge of his denial, and then brought into focus on meeting the risen Lord. The Hebrew for 'Humble' is 'Shach' (שַׁח), a word composed of two letters, Sheen (שׁ: Teeth), and Chet (ח: Wall). According to this word, humbling is when the wall of the inner man is consumed or rather, destroyed. It is in that place where a real child-like dependence on God is cultivated. With this stripping away Simon officially became Peter, a different man, no longer full of himself, but a vessel thirsting to be filled at the outpouring of the Spirit and fit for the Master's use. Here Peter stepped into the destiny for which he was called. He was called and reinstated with a miracle catch of fish (1), admittedly there were hiccups along the way (Jesus' rebuke and Peter's denial of Christ), but now he was ready to throw out the net as a fisher of men (2).

The Hebrew word 'Shach'
which means 'humble'
pictures the walls of
the inner man destroyed

The Council of God

Isaac grew through overcoming natural and spiritual opposition. He discovered a *'broad place'* as he traveled through the three previous wells, then arrived at Beersheba where he cut covenant with Abimelech, Phichol and Ahuzzah. If Isaac's

1) Luke 5:4-7; John 21:6-19; (2) Matthew 4:19; Acts 2:14-41.

association with Abimelech paralleled his relationship with God the Father, what might this say about Abimelech's companions, Phichol, who is described as *'Commander of the army'* and Ahuzzath, who is recorded as a *'friend'*, 'councilor' or 'support in trial'? Ahuzzath is a type of Holy Spirit, who is our advocate and comforter and Phichol represents Jesus Christ, as the Word, who commands and directs the host of heaven. Beersheba means 'Well of the oath' and relates to two parties laying down their lives for the welfare of the other. As such, Beersheba depicts moving into full sonship. It is the place where the whole body, soul and spirit is given to God so that the Father, Son and Holy Spirit live out of, and are given expression through, the individual. This is the domain of the hundredfold return (1). Just as the three men made up Abimelech's governing council, so they represent the council of heaven backing a son as an ambassador of the kingdom. This is a guarantee of the King's dominion, the Son's authority and the Spirit's companionship. Isaac was clinging to the world around him at the outset of the journey, but at Beersheba he portrays a son, confident in God's word, having proven the well of living water within, and having abandoned tenure on this realm to become a true reflection of the one living through him.

(1) Matthew 19:29 cf. Matthew 13:23.

SUMMARY

(1)Both Joseph and David journeyed through considerable opposition to reach their prophetic destinies.

(2) For Joseph:

    (1) Esek was being physically separated from the promise.

    (2) Sitnah was visited with accusations of sexual impropriety = spiritual misconduct.

(3) Rehoboth was found in prison when he interpreted the baker and butler's dreams.

(3) Isaac came to Beersheba accompanied by a heart sacrifice (altar) as a yielded vessel (pitched tent).

(4) Abraham stepped through into Beersheba and called on the Eternal God.

(5) Abimelech means 'father of the king'.

(6) Isaac's relationship with Abimelech was first one of convenience and but it turned into one of union.

(7) Personification is where a person can represent a city, country or virtue, etc.

(8) Rebekah was symbolic of Isaac's spirit. Lying about his wife showed that he and his spirit were not one.

(9) Words from the Spirit of God have the backing of heaven.

(10) Truth (Hebrew: Emet) basically means there is alignment between what's inside and what's outside.

(11) A lie is when you say one thing and your heart says another.

(12) The bursting forth of life-giving revelation is a son's livelihood, but he is prepared for breakthrough by being disquieted.

(13) God's image of a mature son is one who reflects the Father in such likeness and intensity as to make His very essence present.

(14) Beersheba may be summarized by the verse, 'He who finds his life will lose it, and he who loses his life for My sake will find it'.

(15) Abimelech is a type of the Father, Phichol as commander of the army is a type of the Son (Word), Ahuzzath is type of Holy Spirit, the friend and support in trial.

(16) Beersheba is the place of full sonship.

(17) Beersheba is the place of the full council of God: King's dominion, Son's authority, Spirit's companionship.

(18) At Beersheba Isaac abandoned tenure on this realm to embrace heaven as his home.

CHAPTER TEN

Building A Framework

If there were a verse that captured the core teaching of the last chapter it would be,

'I beseech you therefore, brethren, by the mercies of God,
that ye present your bodies a living sacrifice,
holy, acceptable unto God, which is your reasonable service.'
Romans 12:1

The next verse of this passage further exhorts us as New Covenant believers not to be conformed to the world, but rather be transformed by the renewing of our minds (1) so that we may, *prove what is that good and acceptable and perfect will of God.'* There are two main thoughts here:

1) build a different grid through which you view life, and
2) test, validate or prove it.

1) Romans 12:2.

125

This suggests that the kingdom to which we have been brought through Jesus' death upon the cross is radically different from the world that continually feeds our natural senses. For that reason, we need to immerse our hearts in the kingdom and explore its reaches, that once proven, we would be ready to challenge the natural laws when the opportunity arises.

When Jesus came down from the Mount having taught the disciples the precepts and principles of the kingdom He re-entered everyday 33AD life. While His opening moves are profound displays of miracle power, each is also undergirded by an unseen kingdom. Please read Matthew 8:1-9:8.

Seeing the Kingdom Behind the Scenes

The first incident recorded is of a leper coming to Him to be made clean. Jesus performed the leper's request and said to him not to make it widely known, but that he should go and make an offering unto the priest in accordance with the instructions given by Moses in the Law (1). On the surface, an incredible miracle took place and behind the scenes encoded messages were telegraphed. The offering for the cleansing of a leper is to take two turtledoves, put one in an earthen vessel, kill it, and then dip the other bird in its blood before releasing it to spread the message of the cleansing (2). Jesus is that first bird (heavenly being), who was clothed with humanity (an earthen vessel), and killed. The second bird is Holy Spirit, who now spreads the message of mankind's cleansing from sin (leprosy's equivalent). Jesus was not only prophetically

(1) Matthew 8:2-4; (2) Leviticus 14:2-7.

bookending His mission at the commencement of His ministry, but was also sending a cryptic message to the religious hierarchy that their Messiah had come. If they had the ears to hear, it would have triggered their attention to the fact that God was up to something.

Angels

A centurion then comes to Jesus as He enters Capernaum, and states that his servant is paralyzed and in torment at home. Jesus offers to come and heal him. As you know, the centurion answers,

'Lord, I am not worthy that thou should come under my roof:
but speak the word only, and my servant shall be healed.
For I am a man under authority, having soldiers under me:
and I say to this man, Go, and he goes; and to another,
Come, and he comes; and to my servant, Do this, and he does it.'
Matthew 8:8-9

Jesus rightly acknowledges his faith, responds, and the servant is healed that very hour. While most commentators on this passage concentrate on faith in the spoken word, or the need to be under authority to exercise authority, the unseen realm of angels is also at work here. Parallel to his giving orders and his men and servants obeying his commands is recognition by the centurion that unseen agents (angels) are deployed to carry out Christ's word. It could be argued that when Jesus said, *'I have not found such great faith, not even in Israel!'* He may well have been referring to the centurion's understanding of the unseen realm of angelic servants. In commending the centurion He presents a contrast between Abraham, Isaac and Jacob - each of whom acknowledged and encountered angels (1) - with those of their lineage who will be cast out (2).

It should come as no surprise that angels play a major role in the kingdom of heaven. We should have an understanding and appreciation for their roles as they work together with us as sons (3). When Adam F Thompson and I present conferences in understanding the voice of the Spirit, the prophetic, and dream interpretation, we experience evident angelic activity during those times. People repeatedly report and testify to seeing angels as we minister. This is normal kingdom living and it should not be seen as out of the ordinary.

Amongst other things, angels facilitate the word of the Lord (4), they bring deliverance (5), they release revelation (6), they inform and direct (7), they lead into prosperity (8), they are guardians (9), they war against spiritual foes (10), they war against physical foes (11), they strengthen (12), they are end time harvesters (13), they accompany Christ (14), they are assigned to individuals (15), they open doors (16), and they are involved in healing (17).

Dead Men Walking

Incredibly relevant to us and the discussion of the last chapter are events that took place at Peter's house after Jesus healed his

---

(1) Genesis 18:2; 22:11, 15; 24:7, 40; 28:12; 31:1-2; 48:16; (2) cf.Acts 23:8; (3) Hebrews 1:14; (4) Psalm 103:20; (5) Acts 12:7, 11; (6) Daniel 10:14; (7) Matthew 1:2--24; 2:13, 19; 28:5-7; Acts 10:3-8; (8) Genesis 24:40; (9) Psalm 91:11; (10) Daniel 10:13, 20; (11) 2 Samuel 5:24; (12) Daniel 10:18; Matthew 4:11; (13) Matthew 13:39, 49; 24:31; (14) Matthew 16:27; (15) Matthew 18:10; Acts 12:15; (16) Acts 12:10; Matthew 28:2; (17) John 5:4.

mother-in-law of a fever. The passage records that when evening had come they brought to Him many who were demon-possessed and He cast the spirits out with a word, and then healed the sick. What is interesting in the light of Isaac's journey to Beersheba is that Matthew records that these deliverances and healings are the fulfilment of a prophetic word from Isaiah, that He,

> *'Himself took our infirmities and bore our sicknesses.'*
> Matthew 8:17

At this point it needs to be asked, when did Jesus bear our sicknesses? Stop and think about that. The answer is: when He was upon the cross (1). Now this all makes sense because Jesus was ministering in the finished work of the cross BEFORE He had physically given His life upon it. As a Son, He had traversed to Beersheba, and like those before Him, was already dead. As a dead man He could freely avail Himself of heaven's provision.

---

*Jesus was ministering
in the finished work of the cross
before He had
physically given His life
upon the cross!*

In this instance he was ministering deliverance and healing (which is part of a son's provision in the kingdom) based on His sacrifice that was yet to take place. This is also why in replying to

(1) Isaiah 53:4-5; (2) John 2:4.

His mother, who informed Him that they had no wine, He could say, 'Woman, *what do I have to do with you, My hour is not yet come?*' (2), He is actually making reference to His rendezvous with Jerusalem (See earlier page 55). He performed the miracle of turning water into wine not only as a metaphoric declaration and bookend of what would be achieved at the end of His earthly ministry, but was displaying a present access to heaven based on His future sacrificial offering.

> '*When Christ calls a man, He bids him come and die.*'
> Dietrich Bonhoeffer

So, how do you and I access heaven's provision? It's simple, make the journey to Beersheba. The call is to lay our lives down as living sacrifices, before we physically die, and in doing so we completely identify with Christ's death upon the cross, and thereby gain full access to the kingdom. Then like Paul we can say,

> '*I have been crucified with Christ, nevertheless I live,*
> *but Christ lives in me.*'
> Galatians 2:20.

Deliverance Preceded Healing

One last thought on this episode in Peter's house as it relates to the kingdom: Jesus first cast out the spirits before ministering healing (1). Sometimes we are praying for the sick without consideration of the spiritual foothold of the enemy (2). I'm not

---

(1) Matthew 8:16; (2) Ephesians 4:27.

saying that this should become doctrine, because God can and does act sovereignly outside our religious formulas. Neither are demons the root of all sickness. Sometimes it is simply the result of poor health choices. However, it is interesting to note that when God was transitioning His people into the Promised Land, He did use a two-phased approach: He first brought them '*out*' before He brought them '*in*' (1). Spiritual deliverance through the slain lamb preceded any claim to their physical inheritance (2).

Dwellers or Sojourners

Isaac's journey to Beersheba is again brought into focus after Jesus' interchange with the Centurion and a night of ministry in Peter's house. When seeing the crowds drawn to Him, Jesus commands they leave by boat to get to the other side at which time a scribe approaches and declares, '*Teacher, I will follow you wherever You go*'. Jesus responds,

> '*... foxes have holes and birds have nests,*
> *but the Son of Man nowhere to lay his head.*'
>
> Matthew 8:20

Jesus is saying, 'If you want this you will need to become a sojourner'. The ruling cliques - the Herodians (foxes) and religious elite (birds) - had their security tied to this world, but sonship isn't about being focused on living here. As aliens in this world, sons are just passing through. Jesus was not playing games with this scribe entrenched in the religious hierarchy. He knew the buttons

1) Deuteronomy 6:23; (2) cf. Acts 10:38; Matthew 9:5.

to press that would expose the superficiality of the scribe's claimed devotion. His bluntness in exposing people's hearts prompted Him to encourage His disciples afterwards by saying,

'Truly, I say unto you, There is no man that hath left house... or lands, for my sake, and the gospel's, But he shall receive a hundred-fold now in this time, houses... and lands, with persecutions...'

Mark 10:29-30

He did this because contrasted to those practicing some level of religious superficiality there are those who are genuinely making the transition to sonship. These are pilgrims who have made commitment to lose sight of the shore from which they have come, but have not yet fully realized their new life and stepped ashore in the new land.

Authority Above and Under the Earth

With Jesus finally in the boat, He slept as they made their way across the sea. When a great tempest came up, His disciples - some of whom were seasoned fishermen - were really concerned they were going 'down'. So in fear they woke Him, to which He responded, *'Why are you so fearful, O you of little faith?'* (1). When Jesus arose and rebuked the winds and the sea there was a contrasting calm. Accordingly, His disciples marvelled amongst themselves saying, *'Who can this be that even the winds and sea obey Him?'* There are various directions a discussion on this passage could take. Rather than focusing on the fear versus faith aspect,

(1) Matthew 8:26.

which is indeed more than worthy of consideration, let's chew over the wind and the sea for a change. Remember the chapter about creation and how on the fifth day God created the fish and birds? In overlaying sonship in that account, the birds symbolized the spirit realm above the earth, and the fish represented the spirits under the earth. Similarly here, beyond the physical storm, the winds represent spiritual opposition in the heavens and the raging waters, hell's fear-induced fury. Jesus was demonstrating for us how not to be phased by spiritual opposition. Just as Isaac encountered opposition at the first two wells, we are to move on, like him, and draw from the kingdom within. This is especially true when we perceive that Jesus doesn't seem to be moved by our dismay at the opposition against us. He has handed the baton to us as sons, and as sons seated in heavenly places we are to exercise our kingdom authority and hold to the revelation he has given us for that situation.

Piecing Scenes Together

The next episode recorded in Matthew's account is when Jesus stepped out of the boat on the other side and was met by '*two possessed with devils*'. From the outset this is intriguing because the other gospel accounts say that Jesus was met by one man, Legion. Is this a discrepancy? Some believe so and therefore avoid commenting on it. However, I believe it is possible to reconcile the two stories by joining together the different accounts and seeing a bigger picture. All three gospels accounts - Matthew, Mark, Luke - record that Jesus was met by demons who identified Him as, '*Jesus,*

Son of God'. In each account they cry out that He not torment them, but should they be cast out, let it be into the swine feeding nearby.

In Mark's version of events, he also states the man had been crying and cutting himself with stones (1). Luke adds that when the demoniac saw Jesus he fell down at his feet (2), while Mark describing the same event, says that he ran and worshiped Him (3). There is enough 'play' in Matthew's choice of wording to accommodate a composite picture of a man caught in a battle between two worlds: demonic and human. He was indeed two men spiritually (demon and human) and one (the physical man) at the same time (4). This explanation is in line with Matthew's kingdom perspective and better accommodates the end of the story where he was found to be in his *'right mind'* (5).

Legion was a territorial spirit/principality, as is witnessed by the words *'No man might pass that way'* (6). Taking into consideration that Jesus returned to minister (7) in this place, it is understandable why He went out of His way to bring this stronghold down. Strategically, He targeted the strongman in the area, brought peace to his tormented soul, who then in turn became a herald of the kingdom (8). Like modern warfare where mastery of the skies is first priority, Jesus always leads of by establishing spiritual supremacy so that a ground offensive can begin. This is also in line with Jesus' sending out of the twelve where He first gave them authority over unclean spirits (the spirit realm) and then over sickness and disease (the natural realm) (9). Considering the role Legion played in the enemy's camp we can be reasonably certain that the storm faced earlier in the crossing

(1) Mark 5:5; (2) Luke 8:28; (3) Mark 5:6; (4) cf. Matthew 12:26; (5) Mark 5:15; Luke 8:35; (6) Matthew 8:28; (7) Mark 7:31; (8) Mark 5:20; (9) Matthew 10:1.

was a stirring in satan's ranks. Indirectly, this tells us Jesus' detour was deliberate and directed by God (that is, this was no chance encounter), and that the action in the boat was a bigger picture in play. It also informs us that opposition is often a 'heads up' that a significant kingdom breakthrough is imminent.

Finally, Jesus demonstrated how to undertake a successful kingdom offensive. Even though this territorial spirit could not be bound by physical chains it was bound by someone much stronger, simply by encountering the tangible Spirit of God and recognizing the authority of His word (1). Oh, how we need to be bearers of His tangible presence!

Like modern warfare where
mastery of the skies is a priority
Jesus always first established
spiritual supremacy that
a ground offensive may begin

The Kingdom Follows The Cross

In conclusion, Matthew Chapter Nine opens with Jesus returning to His own city where He heals a bed-ridden man of a palsy (2). Like those He healed earlier at Peter's house, this is another example of Jesus applying His death on the cross before its time. And just as He ministered to the person's spirit in deliverance before bringing healing to the body, He applied the same two-fold

(1) Matthew 8:32; 12:28-29. (2) Matthew 9:1-8.

135

approach, here. This passage demonstrates that forgiveness of sins and healing are equal benefits of the Atonement. However, it also reveals that Jesus ministered the healing attributes of the kingdom on the basis of the cross - ' *Arise, take up your bed, and go home*' (1) - after saying, '*Son, be of good cheer; your sins are forgiven*' (2). Without the cross there is no kingdom, and without the kingdom all we have is religion.

An Ongoing Quest

Jesus' acts continue as we read further through the Gospel. As the events unfold it is advisable to ask questions of the surface narrative so that Holy Spirit has opportunity to reveal the kingdom in operation behind the story. To use team sports as an illustration, it is all too easy to become a spectator, even when you are on the field. A spectator is a person waiting for things to happen instead of actively engaging in the action of the game. The same is possible when it comes to reading our Bibles, we can be dulled into passively listening to each story, or we can participate by probing beneath each event and discourse to better understand why things unfold as they do. Always test and prove potential insights through comparison with other Scriptures in order to build a bigger framework of the unseen realm.

Though we are in the world, maturing sons are not of it, and the call upon us is to repeatedly feed our hearts and minds on kingdom truths so that the Kingdom of God becomes more real to us than the matrix of the earthly realm that our senses have conditioned us to.

(1) Matthew 9:6; (2) Matthew 9:2.

```
Kingdom Foundations
  Kingdom Lessons
    Surface Lessons
      Surface Narrative
```

Kingdom Foundations

Having considered this passage of Scripture at a level beyond the surface narrative, to show the kingdom in operation, let us now confirm our earlier discussions on the TSOTM by briefly identifying the kingdom foundations that are its bedrock. Getting to the heart of the matter at this level is not always clear-cut because of individual perspective, overlapping and the multiplicity of characters involved.

The Leper

Leper: 'Blessed are the poor in spirit...'
Jesus: 'Blessed are the merciful...'
Jesus: 'Blessed are those that hunger and thirst for righteousness...'
Priest: 'Blessed are the pure in heart for they shall see God'.
(Jesus revealed they were blind)

The Centurion

Centurion: 'Blessed are the poor in spirit...'
Centurion: 'Blessed are the merciful, for they shall obtain mercy'.
Jesus: 'Blessed are those that hunger and thirst after righteousness...'
Jesus: 'Blessed are the merciful...'

Peter's House

Peter's mother-in-law: 'Blessed are the merciful...'
Jesus (Deliverance): 'Blessed are those that hunger and thirst after righteousness' (1).
Jesus (Healing): 'Blessed are the merciful...' (2).

The Scribe

Scribe: 'Blessed are the pure in heart...' (Jesus revealed the duality in his heart)

In the Storm

Disciples: 'Blessed are the poor in spirit...'
Jesus: 'Blessed are the peacemakers, for they shall be called sons of God.' (3)

Legion

Legion: 'Blessed are the poor in spirit...'.
Jesus: 'Blessed are those that hunger and thirst after righteousness...'
Jesus: 'Blessed are the merciful...'
Jesus: 'Blessed are the peacemakers, for they shall be called sons of God'.
Townspeople: 'Blessed are the pure in heart...'
(They wanted Him out of their region).

The Paralytic

Jesus: 'Blessed are those that hunger and thirst after righteousness...'
Jesus: 'Blessed are the merciful...'

(1) cf. Hebrews 5:13; (2) cf. Psalm 6:2; (3) Romans 8:19.

Regardless of whether we have identified all the individual precepts here or not, there is one thing that stands out from the rest and that is the number of times the fourth and fifth Beatitudes feature as the foundation of kingdom ministry. The reason for this is that these two - righteousness and mercy - are a couplet representative of the heart of God. It is important to recognize here that 'righteousness', 'truth' and the 'word' share common ground because God's word is truth (1), and righteousness is the fulfilment of that truth (2). This is the reason the poetic Scriptures repeatedly focus on God's *'mercy and truth'* (3). A great example of this in operation is when Jesus ministered to the paralytic: the righteousness of God was displayed as He forgave the man his sins (according to the finished work of the cross), and is then backed up with the mercy of God to release healing (according to the Scriptures). Alternatively, the interconnected nature of these two precepts can also see the mercy of God in forgiving the man his sins, followed by the righteousness of God in healing him. The exciting part of this is that the foundation of righteousness and mercy (as the heart of God) is the very same ground on which the cross and the kingdom are laid. Which means that the cross and the kingdom are not only inextricably linked, they are inseparable. You cannot have one without the other.

Without the cross
there is no kingdom,
without the kingdom
all we have is religion

(1) John 17:17; (2) Matthew 3:15; (3) Psalm 25:10; 40:11; 57:3, 10; 61:7; 69:13; 85:10; 86:15; 89:14; 98:3; 100:5; 108:4; 115:1; Proverbs 16:6; 20:28.

SUMMARY

(1) '*And be not conformed to this world: but be ye transformed by the renewing of your mind, that ye may prove what is that good, and acceptable, and perfect, will of God.*'

Romans 12:2

This verse speaks of:
> (1) Building a different grid through which we view life,
> (2) Testing, validating and proving it.

(2) Because the kingdom to which we have been brought is radically different to the realm in which we now live we need to immerse ourselves in it so that it becomes our reality.

(3) Jesus' miracle ministry is undergirded by an unseen kingdom.

(4) Jesus' opening miracle of healing the leper telegraphed a message, and had the religious hierarchy eyes to see it they would have been awakened to God's true heart.

(5) Amongst other kingdom dynamics the encounter with the Centurion also raises our awareness of the partnership sons have with the angelic workers of the kingdom.

(6) It is recorded that Jesus healed in accordance with the word that He, '*took our infirmities and bore our sicknesses*', even before He had physically given His life.

(7) How do we access heaven? Simple, make the journey to Beersheba.

(8) Often deliverance, or the spiritual root of a sickness, needs to be identified and dealt with before healing is manifest.

(9) Not all sickness has a spiritual root, sometimes sickness is the result of poor health choices.

(10) Sons are sojourners passing through rather than dwellers focused on the here and now.

(11) The wind and waves symbolize the spiritual opposition above and under the earth.

(12) Encountering spiritual opposition is a call to hold to the revelation He

has given us for a given situation.

(13) Legion was a man in a battle between two worlds:

    (1) Demonic and human

    (2) He was two men spiritually in one physical body.

(14) Jesus first established spiritual superiority (victory in the air), and then brought physical wholeness (ground offensive).

(15) Opposition is a 'heads up' that a significant breakthrough is imminent.

(16) In Matthew 9:2-6 Jesus used a two-fold approach:

    (1) Sins forgiven (spirit)

    (2) Arise and walk (body)

(17) Without the cross there is no kingdom and without the kingdom all we have is religion.

(18) The cross and the kingdom are inseparable, you cannot have one without the other.

CPSIA information can be obtained
at www.ICGtesting.com
Printed in the USA
FFOW05n1606171217